"*Great Work, Great Career* is an outstanding road map for anyone searching for deeper meaning in their professional life. It provides simple, straightforward ideas to help people discover and develop their talents and abilities to create a great career and, ultimately, achieve their life goals."

—**Diana Thomas,** Vice President, U.S. Training, Learning, and Development, McDonald's

"*Great Work, Great Career* is an insightful, relevant read for anyone seeking to establish a successful career in the current world of work. Covey and Colosimo provide readers with the necessary tools to enjoy long-term workplace satisfaction."

—**Brent D. Peterson, PhD,** coauthor of *Fake Work: Why People Are Working Harder Than Ever but Accomplishing Less, and How to Fix the Problem*

"*Great Work, Great Career* helps you to discover the unique passion, talents, and strengths you have to offer at work and inspires you to contribute and make the difference that only you can make."

—**Marcus Buckingham,** author of *Find Your Strongest Life: What the Happiest and Most Successful Women Do Differently*

Great
Work Great
Career

Stephen R.
COVEY

Jennifer
COLOSIMO

Published by FranklinCovey Publishing, a division of Franklin-Covey Co.

3 1232 00886 7063

ISBN 978-1-936111-10-7

Printed in the United States of America.

Contents

GREAT WORK, GREAT CAREER

*How to Create Your Ultimate Job
and Make an Extraordinary Contribution*

This book is about creating a great career.

You might be saying to yourself, "I don't want to talk about a career, much less a *great* career. Right now I just need a job. I need to eat!"

Well, if you're looking, we're going to show you how to get that great job now. That's the first, short-term step.

But the day will come when you'll want to do more than just eat. And beyond that day will come another day when you look back at your life and take measure of your entire professional contribution to the world.

This book is about today and tomorrow. It's about getting a great job now *and* enjoying a great career for life.

When we say a person has had a great career, what do we mean? That he or she made a lot of money? moved spectacularly up the corporate ladder? became famous or renowned in his or her profession? What about the familiar comment from every movie star on every talk show: "I can't believe I get *paid* for doing this!" Are only a few people entitled to feel that way, but not the rest of us?

And what about you? Are you looking forward to a great career? Would you describe your current career as "great"? When you get to the end of your productive life, will you be looking back on a mediocre career? a good career? a *great* career? And how will you know?

Furthermore, just *how* do you create a great career for yourself?

As coauthors of this book, we are fascinated by these provocative questions. We have been associated in our work for many years as avid students of what it takes to build a great life and career. And we bring two different sets of experiences to the issue, so occasionally, we will speak to you directly in our own voices. We'll

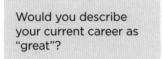

Would you describe your current career as "great"?

share with you our discoveries and provide tools and insights that will help you find answers for yourself. Whether you're looking for a job or want to make the job you have more meaningful, this book is for you.

Anyone Can Have a Great Career

To begin with, anybody can have a great career. It doesn't matter what your line of work is.

It's all in how you define "great career." If you define it as something that brings you a lot of money and power, then you might or might not achieve that "Alexander the Great" level of greatness. Of course, a livable wage is important, but isn't there more to a great career than just a paycheck?

We invite you to think about the most effective, influential people you have ever known professionally. Focus on one face for a moment. It could be the face of a teacher, a co-worker, a friend, or a leader you have worked for. What contribution did that person make to your life? to the organization? to the world? And did it necessarily have much to do with wealth and power?

> A person with a great career makes a distinctive contribution and generates a strong feeling of loyalty and trust in others. Anyone, regardless of title or position or profession, can do these things.

Now, how do you feel about that person? Do you feel a strong sense of loyalty and trust? Do others feel that way?

We believe these are the two key hallmarks of a great career. A person with a great career makes a distinctive contribution and generates a strong feeling of loyalty and trust in others. Anyone, regardless of title or position or profession, can do these things.

Your distinctive contribution is the "what" of your great career. It rises from within yourself, from your unique mix of talents and passions. It is what you alone can create, no matter your line of work.

Loyalty and trust arise from the "how" of your great career. It is the fruit of your character and your conscience, of your highest and best impulses. It comes from doing what you know deep down you *should* do in the way you should do it.

Let us illustrate with one example of a great career.

Fiona Wood was a young English athlete who wanted a career in medicine.[1] She followed the usual track through medical school, married, and while raising six children, completed a specialty in plastic surgery. After moving to Australia, she went to work in Perth at a clinic for the treatment of burn victims.

The agony and scarring suffered by her patients moved her to wonder if there could be better ways to treat them. She knew that the longer a burn takes to heal, the worse the scarring. If only she could speed up the healing process from weeks to days, much of the pain and disfigurement might be avoided.

Her experiments led her to invent "spray-on skin," a method of applying new skin cells over burns. According to Dr. Wood, the technique starts healing in days instead of the weeks needed for conventional skin grafts to work.

Then, on the night of October 12, 2002, her small hospital was flooded with victims of a terrorist bombing on Bali, many of them horrifically burned. Dr. Wood and her small team worked without rest for days and managed to save 25 of their 28 burn patients. Spray-on skin was part of the treatment. This accomplishment brought worldwide acclaim to Dr. Wood, and for the next four years in a row, she was voted in national polls "Australia's most trusted person."[2]

Dr. Fiona Wood clearly shows us what it means to have a great career. It's not the acclaim or the fame, it's the contribution. "You have to push things forward; where there's a need, there's a problem, you have got to find a solution," she says. "In the issue of scarring…we all accepted that if we treated people in a certain way when we operated on them, opened them up, zipped them back up and they had a scar, that was just the way it was. I thought, 'Well, no, it doesn't have to be that way.'"[3]

How could anyone say it more simply? "It doesn't have to be that way." A great career is all about solving great problems, meeting great challenges, and making great contributions.

> A great career is all about solving great problems, meeting great challenges, and making great contributions.

You're probably saying to yourself, "But I'm not a miracle-working surgeon. How can *I* have a great career?" We emphasize that *anyone* can have a great career. Fame, fortune, unusual gifts—these are not the issue.

From Stephen:

A relative of mine has worked for IBM his entire professional life. He has thrived through every transformation of a dynamic company, working hard to stay relevant in an industry that revolutionizes itself every few years. He is very good at his work, which he takes seriously. His clients like him a lot. Even more important, he enjoys a great family life. He is not ambitious in the sense of needing the signs of external success, like constant promotions or public acclaim, but he's making a difference.

To me, that's a great career. He gives the best he has to give, while earning the loyalty and trust of clients, co-workers, and his family.

Many people argue about ambition. Is it a good or a bad thing? I believe it depends on the object of the ambition. If you're ambitious only for the trappings of success and unwilling to pay an honest price for success, ambition can destroy your happiness over time. On the other hand, if you're ambitious to make a real difference — a meaningful contribution — you will experience the deep satisfaction of a job well done and a life well lived. That is the kind of ambition I believe in.

Furthermore, climbing the corporate ladder is not the only way to a successful career. There are meaningful alternatives to "up or out." You define your own great career in terms of what is a "win" for you.

From Jennifer:

I have a French friend who began his career in the automotive industry programming robots to paint cars. He had always been interested in mechanics — cars, bicycles, motorcycles — always taking them apart and putting them back together. At work, he gradually expanded his role as a person who "figures things out" — the only one to fix the unfixable and to make robots do new things. He learned to speak English, a little Italian, and some German so he could better communicate with his global customers and understand their needs in their own words.

Over the years, his responsibility grew until he became manager of a research-and-development team in Detroit inventing new products and solutions. By the time U.S. car companies started to cut costs on robots, he had diversified his group enough to bring in other revenue streams.

In his spare time, he got interested in alternative fuels and converted the family car to run on vegetable oil. He's figured out how to store large quantities so he can take road trips and keep the oil warm in a cold climate. He's always trying to find the cleanest sources of used vegetable oil (typically, from high-end Japanese restaurants). When he drives by, you can smell French fries. Of course, his hobby translates into important contributions at work.

His wife was a top salesperson at the local mall, putting herself through college and earning a marketing degree. After working in research and trade shows, she decided she wanted to be her own boss. She has bought and sold successful franchises, and now works with an organization that promotes nutritional products. She loves helping people solve their health problems and, due to her marketing and selling strengths, has built a very successful business. Having learned French from her husband, she can now offer her product line in France.

My friends do not have famous names. They don't roll in wealth. But they have great, deeply satisfying careers building on their unique talents and passion.

Speaking of their life's work, the French use the word *métier*, which originally meant "ministry" or "service." It's a good word. It contains echoes of giving of the self, ministering to the needs of others, and finding the satisfaction that comes from providing a real and meaningful service. A great career does not rise from a need for outside affirmation, but from within you, from your own curiosity, from your own unique mix of talents and passion.

It also rises from your conscience—from the whispers deep inside that point you to what you *should* do.

Obviously, a person like Dr. Fiona Wood could not make her contribution without gaining the skill to do so. But her conscience is just as key to the making of her great career as her competence is. Those who know her say that her "compassion and deeply held commitment to helping those in need are as important as the technological innovation."[4] Fiona Wood is not just highly capable; she is also a person of high character. Her competence and character together make her a trustworthy person. If you had a severe burn, you would want her treating you.

> A great career requires both of these dimensions—the desire and skill to contribute, and a character worthy of the trust and loyalty of others.

A great career requires both of these dimensions—the desire and skill to contribute, and a character worthy of the trust and loyalty of others.

That means anyone—including you—can choose to have a great career. You can choose to be excellent in your work. You don't need to be a genius or a highly skilled professional like Fiona Wood.

Or, sadly, you can choose a mediocre career and the vague self-disgust that comes with giving less than you are capable of giving. As authors Roger and Rebecca Merrill say, "Mediocre employees are poor leaders, poor team players. They get passed up for pay raises and promotions. They're generally frustrated and bored. They find little or no satisfaction in their work. So why not commit to excellence? You'll contribute more. You'll feel better. You'll make more money. You'll generate more credibility and have greater opportunities."[5]

Furthermore, now is the best of times to start—or re-start—your great career. Something unprecedented is happening, an earthshaking shift in human history that opens undreamed-of possibilities for you.

From Stephen:

My father built a cabin many years ago just outside Yellowstone National Park in the Western U.S.A. It's been part of our family for nearly a century. We love that old cabin with its distinctive smells, overlooking a deep-green canyon lake high in the Rocky Mountains. It's a peaceful place. A cool pine forest reaches down from the amber peaks toward the water. The only sound is the occasional riffle of a fish jumping

But late on a summer night in 1959, this scene was not at all peaceful. A colossal earthquake ripped through the canyon. The lake actually tilted. Family members tell me they heard a great rushing sound of water, but it was so dark out, they couldn't tell if the water was running toward them or away from them. A million trees shattered like sticks. The road broke into huge splinters of asphalt. The mountains cracked, send-ing millions of cubic tons of earth sliding into a nearby river, and another lake appeared overnight.

This mountain oasis is a good place for observing the principles of the natural world at work. Deep beneath this seemingly peaceful land, great geologic forces build up over time and then snap, producing an earthquake that can change the landscape dramatically.

We are now living in such a time, when great forces are converging to produce a new world. The landscape of the economy is undergoing a seismic shift, and with it the landscape of opportunity for each one of us.

These economic "earthquakes" occur periodically in history. The first farmers changed the world massively because they were able to produce a hundredfold more food than the hunters and gatherers who came before them. Then with the machine technology of the Industrial Age came an exponential increase in one worker's ability to produce a hundredfold more than a single farmer could.

Now we're in the middle of another earthquake, an upheaval that changes everything. We're moving from the Industrial Age into the Knowledge Age.

Where a farmer in the Agricultural Age could feed himself and a hundred other people, an Industrial Age worker could provide goods for himself and thousands of other people. But a single worker in the Knowledge Age — what can he or she produce? Where are the limits?

> The landscape of the economy is undergoing a seismic shift, and with it the landscape of opportunity.

There are no limits. And that's the good news about the era we are now entering — the age of knowledge work.

This story will explain what we mean.

Industrial worker Jean got to work at the aircraft plant at 9 o'clock every morning and spent the morning with her rivet gun pounding rivets into the wing of an airframe — same rivet every time. At noon, she ate lunch with her friends. When the whistle blew, she was back at it, spending the afternoon with the rivet gun.

The routine was the same, day after day, year after year. And the same was true for everybody in the company. The accountants made out the same reports. The salespeople called on the same accounts and got the same reorders. At 5 p.m. every day, they all punched a time clock and went home.

Today, Jean's daughter Liz works on that same factory floor, but not at all in the same way. A machine now does the work her mother did. Liz belongs to a cross-functional team, including finance and marketing specialists as well as materials engineers. She invests her day exploring fascinating problems: "How much faster can we produce this composite part? What happens when a new wing skin undergoes wind shear? How can we make the wing spar more damage-tolerant?"

The difference between the Industrial Age and the Knowledge Age is that the world is now calling on you to make the kind of contribution Liz is making. In the Industrial Age, workers were treated like machines. They had "user manuals" called job descriptions. You didn't expect or even want workers to contribute anything unique or unexpected, any more than you wanted a toaster to do something "unique" to your bread.

But a knowledge worker is the opposite of a machine. She chooses the problems she works on. She creates new solutions. She recognizes no limits to the contribution she can make.

A recent news item said the future might not provide enough good jobs for people who want them, as if somehow we're about to run short of exciting problems and challenges demanding answers from creative and curious people.

Obviously, there is no such shortage. Quite the opposite.

Of course, the Knowledge Age is full of turmoil and uncertainty. One daunting consequence of the shift from the Industrial Age to the Knowledge Age is the disappearance of job security. The old lifetime job with a pension at retirement is about finished, and it's probably not coming back. Most Fortune 100 companies are offering new employees only one type of retirement plan: a 401(k) or similar "defined contribution" plan.[6]

In an earthquake, it's hard to keep your footing. You don't know if the water is rushing toward you or away from you.

Still, there is a positive side to this risky but exciting new time: you *can* secure a great future for yourself by becoming an indispensable solution to important problems.

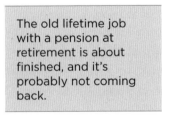
The old lifetime job with a pension at retirement is about finished, and it's probably not coming back.

Instead of pointing with alarm at these developments, we should welcome this wild, complicated new world with passion for the opportunities it presents. There's no shortage of problems, just a shortage of answers.

Begin (or Begin Again) Your Great Career

Maybe now you can glimpse what we mean by a *great* career.

The word "career" comes from the French word *carrière*, which originally meant "going around in a circle," like a car on a circular racetrack. *Carrière* can also mean a "quarry," a place where people go to break rocks all day.

> You are no longer bound by the old mindset that you're just a cog in a machine.

Unfortunately, too many of us experience our careers in this way. We feel like we're going around in circles, getting nowhere. Or we feel like we're hacking away uselessly like prisoners in a rock quarry.

If you feel this way about your career, it's time to rethink everything. You are no longer bound by the old mindset that you're just a cog in a machine, a gear in some great bureaucratic wheel that goes around in meaningless circles. As a thoughtful writer has said, "In the industrial economy, one could do a job with one's body even when the brain and heart weren't committed to the job. But this isn't the case for knowledge work."[7]

The Knowledge Age entices us to ask questions, to challenge old assumptions, to look at the old intractable problems of the world and bring to them our unique answers. It challenges us to look at human need, poverty, misunderstanding, pain, ignorance, and fear and to say to the world, as Dr. Fiona Wood states, "It doesn't have to be that way."

In the Industrial Age, people often found little satisfaction in mechanical work that asked little of them and, as a result, they gave to it as little as they could. But the Knowledge Age changes all of that. You're free to design your own life's work, to unleash your highest and best talents and passions—to make a meaningful difference that literally no one can else can make.

So let us invite you to begin—or begin again—your great career.

This book has two parts. The first part will help you answer the question "What will be your contribution?" The second part will answer the question "How will you make your contribution?" Both parts are essential in building a great career.

Overview of Part 1: What Will Be Your Contribution?

At a point early in his career, the young author Charles Dickens was discouraged. He had a wife and four children to support and another child on the way, and was essentially out of a job. Plagued by self-doubt and mounting financial pressures, he found it hard to write and spent long, sleepless nights walking the streets of London.

As he talked by night with struggling street people, observing firsthand the social strains of child labor, poverty, and hopelessness, an idea formed in his mind. These sights fueled his passion to help the poor, and he began to see beyond his own problems. How could he make a difference? What did he have within himself to contribute to making a better world?

On October 14, 1843, Dickens sat down to write with a renewed zeal. He combined this newfound passion with his genius as a writer to create a small book that he hoped would change the world, as well as his own fortunes. Six weeks later, he published *A Christmas Carol*, an immortal story that at once became wildly popular and transformed public opinion. Some observers connect the beginning of Britain's social reform movement with the publication of the book.[8]

For Dickens, it was also the beginning of a prosperous writing career. His novels made him rich, which enabled him to get involved in educating and reintegrating the poor into society through his Urania Cottage charity.[9]

What was it that recharged Dickens and refocused his great career? He at last found that unique combination of natural talent, passion for a cause, and the call of his conscience to fill a great need in the world.

After counseling with thousands of people seeking to upgrade their careers, we've concluded that what was true for Dickens is true for anyone. It's true for you. It all comes down to finding work that (1) taps your talent, (2) fuels your passion, and (3) satisfies your conscience. But it's not just about you. It's also about answering a significant need.

It's best to start a journey with the end in mind. When you come to the end of your career path and look back, what will you see—a history of great contributions, or aimless mediocrity? The best way to answer that question now is to write what we call a Contribution Statement.

We have always believed in the principle of creating everything twice—first in the mind, then in the physical world. Take building a home, for example. If you're wise, you create a plan before you ever pour the foundation.

You try to get a very clear picture of the kind of house you want before you invest money and energy in building it.

You will spend much of your life and energy on your career, so doesn't it make sense to envision and design a great career for yourself rather than accept what comes by default? That effort starts with your Contribution Statement.

Your Contribution Statement sums up the best you have to offer to the challenges that excite you. It becomes the rudder of your career. With your Contribution Statement in hand, you have the basic direction for your career goals.

> You will spend much of your life and energy on your career, so doesn't it make sense to envision and design a great career for yourself?

Your great career starts, as Peter Hawkins and Nick Smith say, "when you stop asking questions such as 'How do I get promoted?' and start asking 'What is the difference I want to make? What is the legacy I want to leave?'"[10]

Your Contribution Statement is the answer to those questions.

Contribution Statements are highly personal and can take any form. Here are some examples:

- "If someone needs a helicopter to fly higher or faster than it does today, it's up to me to find the materials that can take the heat and stress that kind of performance would put on a helicopter engine." —*Katherine Bicer, materials engineer*[11]

- "[Give] women the message that smart is beautiful...to prevent today's looks-obsessed women from developing eating disorders...to encourage younger women that it's about who you are as a person, not just about how you look."
  — *Dr. Vidushi Babber, physician and educator*[12]

- "Improve working conditions for employees so they suffer from less pain and get fewer injuries while on the job. I would like to do this by creating a positive environment that encourages safety and teamwork." — *Brian Ness, safety engineer*[13]

- Fighting the blight-induced death of Northeast American forests is the career contribution of Jamie Donalds, as he works to restore healthy stands of American chestnut trees: "We all need something to have our life be worthwhile.... This is the difference I want to make."—*Jamie Donalds, orchardist*[14]

- "In corporate leadership roles and over 10 years in coaching and counseling, I discovered the difference I want to make—help people make *their* difference. In doing so, they reclaim their passion and find significance in their work." —*Julia Tang Peters, leadership coach*[15]

One of the best Contribution Statements I've ever seen is a poem written by a young schoolteacher named Taylor Mali, who was once asked by a mercenary-minded friend what she "made" in her teaching job:

You want to know what I make?

I make kids work harder than they thought they ever could....

*I make parents see their children for who they are and
what they can be.…*

I make kids wonder,

I make them question.…

I make them write, write, write,

And then I make them read.…

*Let me break it down for you, so you know what I say is
true:*

I make a difference. What about you?[16]

A great career comes down to making a great contribution, to making a difference that matters to you and to the people you serve. Envisioning, defining, and designing your Contribution Statement is the first step on the path to a great career.

> People who are only looking for a job have résumés. People who are looking to make a great career have Contribution Statements.

The first part of this book will help you develop your Contribution Statement. This is not something you do casually. It requires careful analysis of your own talents, passion, and conscience. You must know your own strengths. It also requires careful analysis of the cause you want to serve and what your employer or customers need from you, as the facing diagram shows. We urge you to take time and give careful thought to writing your Contribution Statement.

I encourage you to write Contribution Statements for every position or project you take on, as well as for your overall career.

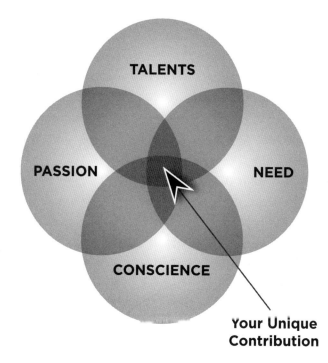

**Your Unique
Contribution**

You have strengths that can't be found anywhere else — a unique combination of your talents, passion, and conscience. Where do your strengths intersect with a compelling market need? At that point lies your ability to make a unique contribution.

People who are only looking for a job have résumés. People who are looking to make a great career have Contribution Statements.

From Jennifer:

Your vision of the contribution you might make will expand, morph, and possibly change outright during your lifetime. I began working when I was 14 years old. I worked some years because I wanted the challenge, the recognition, the opportunity to contribute—and some years because I wanted to eat.

I worked at the counter at Taco Bell and as a grocery-store stocker and cashier, sold prom dresses, waited tables at a Mexican restaurant, and advised members of a health-maintenance organization. My career vision the first seven years of my work life was nothing you'd look at and say, "Wow! How motivating is that?" I had one goal—get a job so I could experience life and break free of the constant struggle to pay the bills.

Maya Angelou said, "You can't be what you can't see." I grew up with very little money in a very small town. My mother graduated from college when I was in high school—the first woman I personally knew who ever finished college—and struggled to do so while raising my brother and me by herself. The idea of leaving town, finishing college, and getting a great job seemed way beyond reach.

Finally, I got my big break when I was selected to teach speech communication as a graduate student. I earned around $10,000 that year. Most of it went to pay for school, so it wasn't the money that was the big break, it was the expansion of my vision—of what I might be able to accomplish and contribute.

Don't get me wrong; I didn't see myself impacting thousands (or impacting anyone, really), and definitely would have laughed you out of the room had you suggested I would coauthor a book with Stephen R. Covey! But in that role, I discovered that I was a good communicator and good with numbers—a unique combination. I found I could take a complex mathematical idea and convey it simply. I could put together an economic analysis and actually explain why people should care about it!

As I became more confident about my own unique contribution, I worked through numerous part-time jobs and internships—improving processes at an auto-parts wholesaler and upgrading workers' compensation at a manufacturing company, among others.

When I interviewed for a culminating job at Accenture, an international business consultancy, the interviewer told me that I knew more about what they did in their change-management practice than he did. Several years at this great company convinced me I could fill an even more rewarding role at FranklinCovey, where I've presented to more than 30,000 people and consulted with clients in 48 American states and 15 countries.

My little vision of independence at age 14 has expanded exponentially, along with my capacity for contribution.

As I identified and capitalized on my strengths, my career Contribution Statement gradually emerged. Still, it changes slightly with every new project, role, and life change. Here's my current Contribution Statement:

I use my economics education and communication strengths as a catalyst for greatness in the FranklinCovey community—for both our clients and the great achievers that work for us globally—by continuously clearing the path for sales and delivery effectiveness.

Overview of Part 2: How Will You Make Your Contribution?

Regardless of the historical, societal, and environmental challenges and opportunities you uniquely face, you have immense choice in what to do *right now*.

Once you have written your Contribution Statement, you will naturally want to make it happen.

Too many people fail to create a great career for themselves because they fruitlessly wait for it to come to them. You hear complaints like these:

- "I don't know where to go to take the aptitude test for that job."

- "I don't know anybody in that company. It's always 'who you know.'"

- "I don't have the education for that job."

- "I don't know how to write a good résumé."

- "I applied for the job, but they never answered me."

We're not saying that barriers don't exist. Each of us must deal with a unique set of disadvantages. In particular, people from an economically disadvantaged background have to overcome many barriers to get to a level playing field. Yet, regardless of the historical, societal, and environmental challenges and opportunities you uniquely face, you have immense choice in what to do *right now.*

Examples abound of people who choose to transcend their disadvantages and make a great contribution. What if the courageous American women's rights advocate Susan B. Anthony had chosen not to campaign for a woman's right to vote and instead spent her life complaining to the women in

> Those who create a great career for themselves are those who make the time to define their contribution and plan how they will achieve it.

her knitting circle? What if the Japanese entrepreneur Konosuke Matsushita, who lost everything in World War II, had chosen not to rebuild the great company known today as Panasonic? What if the world-class Israeli violinist Itzhak Perlman had surrendered to the devastating attack of polio that left him disabled for life?

If you're waiting for someone to take care of you and overcome your obstacles for you, you'll never make the contribution you're capable of. People who get the good jobs are the proactive ones who seize the initiative to get the job done.

Most of us, however, don't face insurmountable obstacles to a great career. For most of us, the issue is time. We are so busy just trying to get through each day, working feverishly at the current job, that we never take the time to map out what we would *really* like to do. Year after year we continue in this unfulfilling cycle, saying to ourselves, "Next year, things will be different. I'll go back to school. I'll start a new career." But then nothing changes. Those who create a great career for themselves are those who make the time to define their contribution and plan how they will achieve it.

The second part of this book will help you with the "how" of your contribution. You'll see how to use your own hidden resources to become a solution for your employer, not just another problem. You'll also discover how to "build a village" of supportive people who value your contribution.

At the end of the book, you'll find answers to Frequently Asked Questions such as these:

- What does a great résumé look like?

- What should I put in a cover letter?

- I know I'm just one of a hundred applicants. How can I bypass the old application run-around and get an interview with the right person?

- What are some ideas for a successful job interview?

- I already have a job, and I need to hold on to it. But I'm not very happy with it. Every day seems about the same. I don't feel like I'm going anywhere careerwise. What can I do?

- It's easy to get a job if you're rich and well connected. But what if I'm just starting out, I have nothing, and nobody knows me?

Each chapter also contains tools to help you apply the insights you gain and build your great career. There's also a special section called "Teach to Learn."

The best way to learn from this book is to teach the content to someone else. Everybody knows that the teacher learns far more than the student. So you're invited to find someone — a co-worker, a friend, a family member — and teach them the insights you've gained. You can follow the "Teach to Learn" guide provided or make up your own.

PART 1

WHAT WILL BE YOUR CONTRIBUTION?

Section Overview

- How to identify your strengths, as summed up by your talents, passion, and conscience.

- How to find a cause you can care about and become indispensable at work.

- How to define your contribution and craft a Contribution Statement.

Know Your Strengths

Your first step in defining your contribution is to know your strengths.

Here are a few penetrating questions you should answer as we ask them:

- Do you feel apathetic at the beginning and the end of the workday?

- Do you feel undervalued or ignored at work?

- Do you hold on to your job in order to keep your insurance and benefits?

- Do you frequently pretend to be busy?

- Do you look forward to your annual performance review with, let's say, something less than excitement?

- Do you find your work meaningless?

And the most important question: *Do you agree that you have more talent, intelligence, capability, and creativity to offer than your current job requires or even allows?*

If you answered yes to any of these questions, you might be caught up in one of the great human dilemmas of our time.

We're referring to the waste of unlimited human potential. We're talking about the possibility that, in your own work, you are simply not allowed to use a significant portion of what you have to offer.

The great philosopher William James taught that "most people live in a very restricted circle of their potential being. We all have reservoirs of energy and genius to draw upon of which we do not dream."[17] Maybe it's time for you to break *out* of that restricted circle of potential being instead of letting the wild times we live in break *you*.

On the other hand, you might not have a job at all and feel unvalued because what you have to offer keeps getting rejected.

In this chapter, we'll talk about how you can know and leverage your strengths to make the contribution only you

> Most people live in a very restricted circle of their potential being. We all have reservoirs of energy and genius to draw upon of which we do not dream.

can make. We'll see how you can literally create your own career by tapping into the highest and best you have to offer.

Here's a story a friend told us:

"I recently spoke with a man not yet 30 years old who graduated from college several years ago with an excellent degree and tremendous talent and energy to contribute somewhere. Today he is employed by a financial-services company.

"I asked him several questions.

"'What is your company's highest strategic priority right now?' He couldn't say.

"'When was the last time you met one-on-one with your manager to talk about your role in achieving the organization's priorities?' He said he hadn't met with his manager one-on-one since his hiring three years before.

"Finally I asked him, 'What have you personally contributed to your organization?' He thought for a moment and quietly answered, 'I've probably saved the company a half-million dollars in the last year.'

"'Who knows that besides you?' I asked him.

"'I make out a report once a week for my boss…but I don't think he reads it.'

"This young man looked crestfallen. I felt deeply for him—his energy had drained out of him, his vigor was gone, his dreams of making a great contribution had shrunk down to fulfilling a mere job description. He had allowed himself to be reduced to a 'job description with legs.'"

Some of the blame for this young man's situation lies with weak management; but to a great extent, he let it happen to himself.

He has lost track of his own worth.

The Singular, Irreplaceable *You*

At the core, there is one simple, overarching reason why so many people remain unsatisfied in their careers. It stems from an incomplete paradigm of *who they are*—*their fundamental view of themselves.*

Your value as a human being is not outside yourself—it comes from inside. Deep down, you must know that you are a being of virtually infinite potential and, unlike a machine, you have the power to choose what you will be.

Too many of us base our self-worth on externals, on being compared to other people.

So many people equate their self-worth—or the worth of what they achieve—to money.

If 30 years of data is to be believed, studies continue to show that salary is actually not as motivating to people as making a contribution they themselves believe in. Salary is an expectation, not an incentive. We rightly expect to be paid fairly if we are performing. Still, one researcher concludes, "It is quite common for someone to be getting an excellent salary and benefits...to hate every minute of their job. Some of these individuals quit that job and take one with lower salary and worse benefits because it is motivating to them.... Most people will spend a lot of time after work and on weekends working for no pay, and often working a lot harder than they do at their regular job, to do something that will be appreciated." [18]

Some people have been socialized by constantly comparing themselves to others to the point that the locus of their identity moves from themselves to other people's opinions of them—to how well they stack up. They lose their identity. This is true "identity theft." They become incapable of making a unique contribution because they have devalued and lost what is uniquely worthwhile about themselves.

The great British management theorist Charles Handy says, "We can define [success] as keeping up with our neighbors...but that answer has a no-win, nightmarish touch if we take it seriously."[19]

In all of the vast universe, there is no one else like you. You are absolutely unique. Your particular combination of strengths, experiences, talents, and ingenuity has never existed anywhere else and will never, ever be repeated. Therefore, no one else can make the unique contribution you can make.

After years of feeling vaguely unfulfilled in his work for oil companies and universities, Charles Handy realized that he was not making the contribution he was capable of. He took an inventory of his unique talents and passions and decided to start a new story in his career.

He recounts: "I woke up early on the morning of... my forty-ninth birthday. Not usually a landmark event, one might think, but I was drowsily aware that this time the cliché was true; today really was going to be the first day of the rest of my life.... I would be unemployed—by my own choice. I didn't call it unemployed, of course. I was 'going portfolio' I would say."[20]

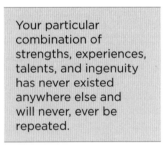

Your particular combination of strengths, experiences, talents, and ingenuity has never existed anywhere else and will never, ever be repeated.

Handy was not really unemployed; he still had plenty of meaningful work ahead of him and many clients to serve. He had simply changed his mindset. He no longer saw himself as just another gear in an organizational machine, but as a "portfolio of strengths"—a combination of assets unique to himself, like a portfolio of stocks and shares. Among these assets were his unusual grasp of economics and his native, plainspoken writing ability. Since then, he has written 18 remarkable business books and made an astounding contribution to the whole world of business.

Handy tells of a conversation he had with a friend, a "forty-eight-year-old advertising executive who was complaining that there were no longer any jobs in the age-ist advertising world for older people like him." But Handy knew that was the future: fewer and fewer jobs "where you sold your time in advance, usually years in advance, to an organization." So Handy encouraged his friend to "go portfolio" as he had done.

Changing your mindset in this way doesn't necessarily mean you leave your job. It might mean that; but more precisely, it means waking up to what you can truly contribute instead of passively living out someone else's idea of your job description.

Professor Richard Florida observes that "our economy is in the midst of a fundamental long-term transforma tion—similar to that of the late 19th century, when people streamed off farms and into new and rising industrial cities. In this case, the economy is shifting away from manufacturing and toward idea-driven creative industries."[21] This new economy is unpredictable and disorienting. New technologies blossom overnight, while long-established companies wither away just as quickly. In the Knowledge Age, creativity and contribution matter most.

In the Industrial Age, people simply asked, "What's my job description?" Now, according to Peter Drucker, "Knowledge Age workers must learn to ask, 'What should my *contribution* be?' This is a new question in human history. Traditionally, the task was a given. Until very recently, it was taken for granted that most people were subordinates who did as they were told. The advent of the knowledge worker is changing this, and fast."

Working in the Knowledge Age with the old paradigm of the Industrial Age leads nowhere. Passively carrying out a job description in the turbulent realities of this new world can quickly leave you irrelevant, stranded on the sidelines. Why? Because your job description is obsolete the moment it's written. If you are not constantly changing to adapt to the challenges your organization faces, you'll be left behind. As philosopher Hsing Yun observes, "There simply is nothing to which we can attach ourselves, no matter how hard we try. In time, things will change and the conditions that produced our current desires will be gone. Why then cling to them now?"[22]

> Knowledge Age workers must learn to ask, "What should my *contribution* be?"

If you have an Industrial Age paradigm, you see yourself as a tool used by others. On the other hand, if you have a Knowledge Age paradigm, you see yourself as a solution provider who brings a singular set of tools to solving significant problems.

Industrial Age Paradigm	Knowledge Age Paradigm
"I am my function."	"I make a significant contribution."
"I'm a job seeker."	"I'm a problem solver."
"I'm a gear in an organizational machine."	"I am a human being with a portfolio of unique strengths—talents, passion, and a conscience."

The difference between the Industrial Age paradigm and the Knowledge Age paradigm is fundamental. It's the difference between a passive person with no initiative and an active person who takes responsibility for the future.

Yet, many are not willing to make the mental transition away from the Industrial Age mindset. As a result, the *Times of London* reports, "Many workers are so ill at ease in the office that they spend a large part of the day simulating work. That generates more negative stress than excessive working. The result is serious but hidden depression in the office."[23]

Adopting a Knowledge Age paradigm means that you bring your individual portfolio of strengths to relevant, meaningful problems and challenges. You are not a "job description with legs." You are a knowledgeable, skilled, proactive, thinking, and creative human being with unlimited potential; and you can leverage that portfolio of strengths to make your own unique contribution.

Identify Your Portfolio of Strengths

A key step is to identify a portfolio of strengths you can leverage. At the end of this chapter is a tool that will guide you in identifying your strengths. These

> You are not a "job description with legs."

strengths can be divided into three categories: your talents, your passion, and your conscience.

Why these categories?

Because they sum up what you *are*—not just what you do. You are more than just a bundle of capabilities; that would make you a machine. You are more than just your passion and instincts: that would make you merely an animal. And a key distinction is your conscience—the part of you that whispers what you *should* do with your life, what your *responsibility* is. Your talents, passion, and conscience together add up to a whole person. Unless you are invested as a whole person in your career, you will always find yourself underemployed, frustrated, and perhaps burdened with guilt.

Career advisors who say "Do what you love" are only partly right. Doing what you love might not be enough to make you marketable, nor will it always satisfy your conscience. Someone has to be willing to pay you to do what you love.

> Your talents, passions, and conscience together add up to a whole person.

And there are aspects to every great career that are not necessarily "loveable," but which must be done.

Those who say "go with your strengths" usually mean "go with your talents and abilities." But you are strong in more than just your talents and abilities. You have a strong passion. You have fervor for some things that would bore other people. Your passion is just as important to the whole equation as your capabilities, as is your conscience.

Now, please give serious thought as you answer the key questions under each of these categories.

Talents

First, let's consider your talents.

- What unique knowledge, talents, or skills do you have that can help you make a contribution?

The category of talent is all about the tools you carry with you. In the Industrial Age, the company owned the tools and the means of production; the talents of individual workers were pretty much irrelevant. That's not so anymore. In the Knowledge Age, as Peter Drucker says, we each literally own "the means of production.... Those means are in our heads and at our fingertips.... Intelligence has become the new form of property. Focused intelligence, the ability to acquire and apply knowledge and know-how, is the new source of wealth."[24]

"Here's the good news," says Charles Handy. "It is almost impossible to stop people from getting [intelligence]. In theory, anyone can be intelligent in some way or can become intelligent and thereby have access to power and wealth. There is little to stop a small firm muscling in on Microsoft's territory just as Microsoft did to IBM. When the key property is intelligence, you do not have to be big or rich to get in on the act. It is a low-cost entry marketplace."[25]

Talents are like fingerprints. Everyone has them, and no two are alike. Your talents are unique to you.

Now, don't confuse your skills with your talents. People can have skills where their talents do not lie. If your job requires your skills but not your talents, you will never tap into the genuine and instinctive part of yourself.

> Intelligence has become the new form of property. Focused intelligence, the ability to acquire and apply knowledge and know-how, is the new source of wealth.

There are all kinds of talent tests and personality profiles out there that can help you identify your talents, and they can be good tools to have in a portfolio. But be careful. Most of them fit you into some category or another. You're an "influencer." You're a "relator." Or a "yellow" or a "blue" or a "diamond" or a "heart" or a "club." The results generally point to some function you might carry out well, such as "facilitator" or "creator." They actually plot you on a graph as if you were a number.

Beware of getting pigeonholed in this way. The danger is you'll start to think of yourself as destined for one function or another—that you'll *identify* yourself with your function.

From Jennifer:

I once took a group of 12-year-old Girl Scouts to do a service project at a food bank. There we met a gentleman who was clearly a maintenance worker. He stopped sweeping the floor long enough to tell the girls that he hoped that one day they would be able to find a job that made as big a difference to the world as his did. He shared with us how proud he was to "feed the hungry." This man did not just have a function. He was making a contribution.

From Stephen:

I know of a first-class choir director. He has taught choruses in public schools; he conducts church choirs; he composes and arranges beautiful music. He has been organist for a magnificent church in Los Angeles. But he is also fascinated by law, and did well in law school. Today he combines his unique capabilities in law and music as legal counsel to one of the great recording companies in the music industry. No pigeonholing survey could have placed him in this position.

Although the results can be interesting and, no doubt, can give you insights, most talent or aptitude tests are relics of the Industrial Age. The better ones describe your attributes and traits so that you can discern multiple sources of strength in yourself. The key to their usefulness is a fundamental shift in thinking: you need to seriously reflect on the kind of contribution you want to make rather than the kind of function you want to have.

You are *not* your *function*.

- The industrial worker says, "I want to be a microbiologist." *This is a function.* (Of course, you must be educated in microbiology if you hope to contribute to the field, but the word "microbiologist" does not define you.)

- The knowledge worker says, "I have an inquisitive nature. I'm persistent and painstaking and very much at home in the biolab. I want to use these talents to help develop food plants that are more resistant to disease." *This is a contribution.*

Not even the best talent test can tell you about your *uniqueness*. The knowledge worker above goes on to say, "I grew up knowing about plants. Other kids knew about athletes or music. I knew the scientific names of dozens of different tomato plants. I could tell you which tomatoes were good for sauce, for processing, or for eating. I guess I was a little odd."

Thank goodness, every one of us is a little odd in some way like this. We all know people for whom something comes easily or naturally. You know the gardener who unfailingly grows the most beautiful flowers. You've seen the athlete whose grace and power just flow from her. We know a man who never makes a spelling error. He can spell any word he hears without hesitating.

> Everyone has a unique gift — often we have several. It seems to be a natural principle. So what comes naturally to you?

Everyone has a unique gift — often we have several. It seems to be a natural principle. So what comes naturally to you?

Think about it.

- What do you do easily and well?

- What do people ask you to do because you're good at it? (Whether or not you like what you do well — that we'll deal with later.)

- If someone were to ask your boss or co-workers to list your talents, what would they say?

Management consultant Richard Koch gives this advice: "It's important to focus on what you find easy. This is where most motivational writers go wrong. They assume you should try things that are difficult for you.... You are already successful at some things, and it matters not a whit if those things are very few in number. The 80/20 principle is clear. Pursue those few things where you are amazingly better than others and that you enjoy most."[26]

Passion

Enjoying your career is just as important as using your talents, and that brings us to the category of passion. Answer this question thoughtfully:

- What job-related opportunities are you passionate about?

Never downplay your own passion. Your passion is what fulfills you. It's a fire that comes from within, not from without. Think about times when you were so passionate about a project, you couldn't think about anything else. Did you need to be supervised? Of course not. The idea of being told what to do, and when and how to do it, would have insulted you.

Of course, your passion and talents don't necessarily connect. Our friend who never makes spelling errors doesn't really care about spelling. He has no energy for editing or proofreading or any of the work a perfect speller might be good at.

But often you will *find* your talents through your passion. Back in the 1940s, a young American, Julia Child, found herself living in Paris because of her husband's job. There she discovered a passion for French cuisine and a talent she never knew she had.

On her arrival in France, she had lunch in a little restaurant at Rouen. That first meal of oysters and sole meunière was a revelation to her, like nothing she had ever experienced before. It

> Your passion is what fulfills you. It's a fire that comes from within, not from without.

was "absolute perfection. It was the most exciting meal of my life." She became fascinated by truffles and pâtés and cheeses and wines—"wrestling with the subject of butter in sauces"—everything stirred her interest.

Pursuing her passion, Julia applied to the finest school for chefs in Paris, Le Cordon Bleu. "By now I knew that French food was it for me. I couldn't get over how absolutely delicious it was. My friends considered me some kind of a nut....They did not understand how I could possibly enjoy doing all the shopping and cooking and serving. Well, I did!"[27]

> Your natural passions will boil to the surface one way or the other.

Julia Child spent her professional life joyously producing cookbooks and teaching on television the style and tradition of classic French cuisine. Her contribution to the world as a passionate teacher of this great tradition is unparalleled.

Although Julia Child discovered her passion and her talents as an adult, they were probably always there, just under the surface, waiting to be expressed.

Yellowstone Park is famous for its geysers and sputtering hot springs. Deep beneath the park is a "hot spot" in the Earth's crust, a massive upwelling of molten rock that heats the ground water. The boiling water then finds its way through cracks in the ground and shoots into the sky.

Like these hot springs, your natural passions will boil to the surface one way or the other. Even as a child, you were captivated by certain things. Watch small children sometime. You can see that one is athletic and can't get enough of basketball or football, and another one loves to draw on anything that's available. Another sits quietly and reads in a corner armchair for hours at a time. Another perks up whenever food is mentioned and wants to know exactly how every dish is made. It's easy to see that among them there will someday be coaches, cooks, teachers, and artists, if they can discover and value and build on these strengths in themselves.

Somewhere within you is that simmering well of excitement that needs an outlet.

Here are some questions to think about that will lead you to a better understanding of your passion:

- What do you spend your free time on?
- What do you get energized about? What do you feel like arguing about?
- What do you read?
- What did you do as a child that intrigued you?
- What "Julia Child-like" experiences have you had that excited you?

Conscience

Once you've defined your passion, you need to examine your conscience.

The category of conscience surprises some people. Why do we ask you to listen to your conscience as you build your great career? Because your conscience, your moral compass, will whisper to you and tell you what contribution you *should* make. So answer this question very thoughtfully:

- What is your *real* responsibility to your organization, your customers, and your co-workers?

What a powerful question! Your answer will immediately show you how limited your job description is compared to the contribution you could make.

Is it ethical to hold back what you *can* give, just because it might not be in your current job description?

The renowned management thinker Jim Collins says, "One notable distinction between wrong people and right people…is that the former see themselves as having 'jobs,' while the latter see themselves as having *responsibilities*. Every person should be able to respond to the question 'What do you do?' not with a job title, but with a statement of personal responsibility."[28]

Your conscience tells you what your responsibility is.

Your conscience might even be the source of your greatest contribution. Consider the example of a 16-year-old fast-food worker who blogged about the conditions in the restaurant where she worked. "That place was all about getting your food fast. And that's all they really cared about, even if it meant using old food, dropped food, or the wrong sandwiches. No one really cared about the customer, and that hurt me because I did care. When I took just a little longer to do things right, I would get screamed at for taking too long. Finally I had enough of it and decided to change. I no longer cared about being yelled at. I just worried about doing what was right, how it should be done."

> Every person should be able to respond to the question "What do you do?" not with a job title, but with a statement of personal responsibility.

This courageous young worker made a real difference to the quality of customer service, making a contribution motivated by conscience.

Ultimately, your career has no meaning unless your conscience drives you. If the work you do bothers your sense of integrity or honesty, no other success will make up for your disappointment in yourself. On the other hand, if the work you do satisfies your conscience, then no matter what it is, you will always enjoy peace of mind and a sense of personal fulfillment.

From Stephen:

Personally, I remember the internal struggle I faced as a 50-year-old university professor in deciding to leave the comfort zone of university professorship to set up my own business. If it weren't for the vision of some greater good I might do, I could never have brought myself to make the sacrifice. For me, it was a question of conscience.

Once, as I got into a cab outside a Canadian hotel, the bellman told the driver to "take Dr. Covey to the airport." The driver assumed I was a physician and began to talk about his medical problems. I tried to explain that I wasn't that kind of doctor, but his English was limited and he didn't understand me. So I just listened.

He told me about his aches and pains and his double vision. The more he talked, the more I was convinced that his problems were due to a bad conscience. He complained about having to lie and cheat his way through the system to get fares. "I'm not gonna follow the rules. I know how to get those fares." Then his expression sobered. "But if the policemen find me, I will get in trouble. I will lose my license. What do you think, Doctor?"

I said to him, "Don't you think that the main source of all these tensions and pressures is that you're not being true to your conscience? You inwardly know what you should do."

"But I can't make a living that way!"

I talked to him about the peace of mind and wisdom that comes from living true to your conscience. "Don't cheat. Don't lie. Don't steal. Treat people with respect."

"You really think it would help?"

"I know it would."

As he dropped me off, he refused my tip. He just embraced me. "I'm gonna do that. I already feel better."

Whether you're a cab driver or a cook or a CEO, your career can be great if you give the highest you have within you. You will not be spared difficulties or challenges, but you will experience deep fulfillment as you share the best of your talents, the strongest of your passions, and the commitment of your conscience.

"Know Your Strengths" Tool

These questions will help you identify your strengths in three areas: Talents, Passion, and Conscience. Your responses will be important to writing your Contribution Statement (coming up in the "Contribute Your Best" chapter).

Take time with each question. Pose the questions to others who know you — friends, boss, co-workers.

1. Talents

- What unique knowledge, talents, or skills do you have that can help you make a contribution?
- What do you do easily and well?
- What do people ask you to do because you're good at it?
- If someone were to ask your boss or co-workers to list your talents, what would they say?

2. Passion

- What job-related opportunities are you passionate about?
- What do you spend your free time on?
- What do you get energized about? What do you feel like arguing about?
- What do you read?
- What did you do as a child that intrigued you?
- What job-related experiences have you had that excited you?

3. Conscience

- What is your real responsibility to your organization, your customers, and your co-workers?

Teach to Learn

The best way to learn from this book is to teach the content to someone else. Everybody knows that the teacher learns far more than the student. So find someone — a co-worker, a friend, a family member — and teach him or her the insights you've gained. Ask the provocative questions here or come up with your own.

- Do you think most people have more talent, intelligence, capability, and creativity to offer than their jobs require or even allow? Explain your answer.

- Do you feel like your job requires the best you have to give — the best of your talents and passion and conscience? Why or why not?

- In the Industrial Age, people simply asked, "What's my job description?" Now, according to Peter Drucker, "Knowledge Age workers must learn to ask, 'What should my contribution be?'" What does Drucker mean by this observation?

- Most people think of their talents and skills as their career strengths. Why does it make sense to include their passion and their conscience as career strengths?

- Most people think of their jobs in terms of the function they serve — salesperson, executive, technician, nurse, and so forth. What's the difference between fulfilling a function and making a contribution?

- Jim Collins says, "Every person...should be able to respond to the question 'What do you do?' not with a job title, but with a statement of personal responsibility." What does this statement mean to you? What are you responsible for?

Discover Your Cause

Let's listen to some voices:

- "I've lost my job. Now what do I do?"

- "I've consistently moved up the corporate ladder, but I don't really feel excited about or engaged in my work."

- "I've been here 18 months, and it feels a little like jail. The job certainly isn't what I thought it would be. I'm not sure who is more bored—me or the customers."

- "I put 20 years into that company, and in one afternoon, it's all over."

- "My job is meaningless and I could easily be replaced by a robot."

- "I've been looking for a job for eight months. I'm still upbeat. I know I have a lot to offer. But after hearing 'We're not hiring right now' a hundred times, I'm starting to take it personally."

Maybe yours is one of these anxious voices.

Our unpredictable times have undoubtedly affected you too. You might have lost your job. You might be nervous about keeping your job. You might feel stuck in a job that means little to you.

In this chapter, we'll talk about the secret to getting and keeping the job you want. We'll talk about making yourself indispensable. We'll talk about *discovering your cause.*

The Fire

In the summer of 1988, Yellowstone National Park caught fire. At first, no one worried; forest fires in Yellowstone are common and usually burn themselves out. But this one was different. Drought, wind, and excess fuel in the form of old trees and undergrowth combined to create a perfect firestorm. By summer's end, more than a million acres had burned, and it seemed that Yellowstone—that jewel of a national park—had been destroyed forever.

But it wasn't so. Within a year, baby green pines carpeted the blackened landscape, and today—only a couple of decades later—fresh, new forests have taken over. It turns out that only the heat of fire can stimulate the famous lodgepole pines of Yellowstone to reseed themselves. As part of the natural order of things, the fire did not damage the park; it renewed the park.[29]

Dr. Bernie Siegel has said, "If you watch how nature deals with adversity, continually renewing itself, you cannot help but learn."

The 21st-century economy is giving everyone a wild ride. It seems that turbulent times are here to stay. The seismic shift to a Knowledge Economy has so disoriented many people that they have a hard time getting their footing. Some see only disaster, as if—like the Yellowstone fire—the future is turning to ashes. They see only millions of jobs gone up in smoke, whole industries laid to waste, an economic landscape barren and scarce.

To others, the landscape has never been greener. The volatile, burned-over economy of the new century provides opportunities no one ever dreamed of in industries that didn't even exist a few years ago. What seems to some a disaster holds the seeds of renewal for others. Have the problems of the world gone away? Does the world still cry out for energetic, intelligent people to do its work? Of course it does.

You might be making all kinds of excuses to yourself about your career situation—and some of your excuses are correct! "The economy is lousy. I have no resources. I don't have the education, the background, the connections to make the kind of career for myself that I want to have." But they are all still excuses.

Regardless of the economic climate, so much depends on the paradigm, or mentality, that governs your thinking and actions. If you have a scarcity paradigm, you see only burned ground around you—sparse opportunities, limited possibilities. On the

> The landscape has never been greener. The volatile, burnedover economy of the new century provides opportunities no one ever dreamed of.

other hand, if you have an abundance paradigm, you see prospects springing up everywhere.

Scarcity Paradigm	Abundance Paradigm
"Nobody's hiring. Companies are shedding employees, not adding them."	"Companies have more challenges to meet and problems to solve than ever before. The opportunities for problem solvers are endless."
"Thousands of people are competing for the few jobs out there. I have no resources and no connections. What chance do I have?"	"With my unique strengths and hidden resources, I can create rich and satisfying career opportunities for myself. No one else can do what I can do."
"Only meaningless, dead-end jobs are available. I guess I'll have to settle for that."	"If I can't find a job that leverages my talents and fuels my passion, I'll create one!"

The difference between the scarcity paradigm and the abundance paradigm is fundamental. It's the difference between a victim and the person who takes charge of life. Those with the abundance paradigm know that it's time to talk about the possibilities — not the impossibilities!

We've never had such opportunity as we do today. Turbulent times offer the chance, the opening, the break people have been looking for. If you're let go from your job, you're free to change everything. It is not a time to mope, but a time to get creative. People with the scarcity mentality are too much a product of their conditions rather than their decisions. There are two sides to losing a job, only one of them negative; the positive side is that you're suddenly free to create your own future.

Just look at Steve Demeter of San Francisco, who used to work on ATMs for a big bank. When he got interested in programming applications for the iPhone, he created Trism, a game he sold on the Internet for five dollars per download, and made a quarter-million dollar profit in two months.

At 29, Steve became a millionaire. Leaving the job behind was all upside for him. All he needed was his talent and the time to capitalize on it.[30]

When Ethan Nicholas heard about Steve Demeter, he went on the Internet and learned how to create games for the iPhone as Steve had done. At age 30, Ethan had overwhelming medical bills from the birth of his son and couldn't make his mortgage payments. Within a year, more than two million people had downloaded his iShoot game, and he was making as much as $35,000 a day.[31]

> Although you must make a living, your great career doesn't have to center on money.

Although you must make a living, your great career doesn't have to center on money. One night Kathy Headlee Miner dreamed that she was in Africa, surrounded by women and children, and somebody asked, "Who are you?"

"We are mothers without borders," Kathy answered. She awoke, wondering what that dream was about. Now, years later, she heads a nonprofit company she founded called Mothers Without Borders. Each year she travels to Africa with container-loads of clothing and medical and school supplies for orphans.

On her first trip to Zambia, Kathy interviewed more than a thousand children orphaned by AIDS, many of them living in the streets. Her photo albums tell many stories. "Here's Rachel, with her two siblings. The inside of their one-room house was strewn with garbage. There were flies and maggots everywhere, and they hadn't eaten in three days. Rachel takes in laundry to make a little money, but she doesn't get more than a dime a load."

For such children, a pencil and a pair of shoes may make all the difference in their ability to go to school and get an education to lift themselves from poverty. Kathy has founded an entire village just for children where they can be schooled and cared for. For Kathy, it's a full-time career to nurture children in another hemisphere.[32]

Now, the stories of Steve Demeter, Ethan Nicholas, and Kathy Headlee Miner are unusual. But they symbolize the green fields that are all around you if only you're willing to change your paradigm from scarcity to abundance. And while there's a lot of pain associated with uncertain times, there's also a tremendous range of new possibilities and wonderful satisfactions that weren't there in more placid times.

Most of us probably won't be starting our own businesses launching iPhone games or child-rescue operations. But plenty of existing businesses still need your energy and talent. Yes, hundreds or thousands of others may be competing for those jobs. And the job you already have might be in danger. You can sit around and lament this situation, or you can act.

So let's talk about how to save or get the job you want by completely rethinking that job.

Here are two key mindsets you'll need:

- First, become a volunteer, not an employee.
- Second, become a solution, not a problem.

Become a Volunteer, Not an Employee

Stop thinking about "getting a job" and start "volunteering for a cause." A job is something you do for money. A cause is something you work at because you believe in it. People used to talk about their vocations, not their careers. The term *vocation* literally means "calling"—a cause you are driven to serve based on a deep commitment and a conviction that it's worthwhile.

So change your mindset. Don't think of yourself as an employee but as a *volunteer*. Where an employee has a *job description*, a volunteer has a *cause*. The difference between a job description and a cause is clear. A job description is external, and the employee reactively accepts it. A cause is internal, and you proactively volunteer for it. The motivation for a job comes from *outside* you, while the motivation for a cause comes from *within* you.

Interestingly, nobody ever fires a volunteer. For one thing, a volunteer won't go away. And for another thing, a volunteer's passion and energy are really valuable to any employer. A volunteer doesn't make decisions based on fear or the desire to be important. A volunteer makes decisions based on the right thing to do to get the best result.

One difference between a great career and a mediocre career is finding a cause you can volunteer to serve. We're not talking about earth-shaking causes like solving world hunger or curing cancer. We're talking about any worthwhile cause, regardless

> Where an employee has a *job description*, a volunteer has a *cause*.

of your profession. Until you see your work as a cause, you won't find the passion for it that marks a great career.

Some years ago, a teacher named James Asher became frustrated with the way foreign languages were taught in schools. Most teachers used the "talking head" approach, which Asher described this way: "Students come into a classroom, sit down quietly in rows, and then make 'noises' with their mouths on cue from a person in front of the class who points at a student and says, 'Listen to what I say and repeat after me!'" He felt foolish using this method, which to him was virtually useless.

James Asher became passionately devoted to a cause: to help people learn new languages quickly and easily. He began experimenting with new methods. One of these methods was to give students commands, which they would then act out, such as:

- Stand up.
- Walk to the cabinet. Open the drawer of the cabinet and look for a bottle of aspirin. Pick up the bottle.
- Close the drawer and walk quickly to Mary.
- Offer her the bottle.
- Mary, take the bottle from him and...

Amazingly, English-speaking students learning Russian picked up these commands quickly and *retained* them. Soon they were learning hundreds of new expressions in record time. Asher's discovery, now known as the "Total Physical Response Method," made learning a second language fun, active, and easy.[33]

Inventing a new and better way of teaching languages was not in Asher's job description. He volunteered to do it. To him it was a compelling problem that needed a solution, and it became the cause he has served throughout his professional life.

What about you? What do you want to sign up for?

Obviously, you need to be a *useful* volunteer, equipped with solutions your employer needs. And, of course, you become more useful the more you know about your organization, your industry, and the challenges of the business. We'll talk about these topics in the next chapter. But first, you should have the mindset of a volunteer, not just a job seeker.

Become a Solution, Not a Problem

Listen to the people who are hiring. "Don't come asking for a job," they say. "Bring me a solution!"

Become a *solution* for your employer, not a problem. Adopt a solution mindset. Especially in tough times, your employer or prospective employer doesn't lack problems to solve and challenges to meet. So stop thinking that *opportunities* are lacking—they're not. They're everywhere. It's only the scarcity mentality that gets in the way. The "we're not hiring" message so many companies put out is simply not true. They are hiring—they *will* hire—and they will hire you if *you* are the best solution to a problem they *must solve.*

> Your employer or prospective employer doesn't lack problems to solve and challenges to meet. So stop thinking that *opportunities* are lacking—they're not.

Today, it isn't enough to simply copy and paste company addresses into a generic cover letter. When you submit a résumé or an application, it likely goes into a black hole with perhaps hundreds of other résumés and applications. In fact, many employers have cut back on advertising jobs online, not because they don't have open positions, but because they are overwhelmed with applications.[34] Most people look for jobs with a shotgun instead of a heat-seeking missile. They don't really know what they want, so they send out a bland, passive résumé and come across as bland and passive in employment interviews. They have no

> The most important tool you can have today in business is insatiable curiosity. The minute you lose it, you're dead.

cause to serve except a sort of aimless need for a job.

If you're this kind of job applicant, you're just another problem for the employer. You've become one more person they somehow have to deal with.

As marketing strategist David Meerman Scott points out, "Basically, the old rules of job searches required you to interrupt people to tell them that you were on the market and to coerce them to help you." Scott likens a traditional résumé to a product brochure with you as the product.[35] Unless the prospect is actively looking for just that product, the brochure goes into the bin.

So how do you become a solution instead of a problem? How *do* you become a heat-seeking missile directed at a real target?

The most important thing you can do is to truly become a *knowledge* worker. This means you must gain profound knowledge about the needs you feel called on to serve. Obviously, to gain that kind of knowledge, you must really *research* the company you want to work for—or, if you're trying to save your job, the company you *already* work for. It's not an exaggeration to say that getting the job you want is 90 percent research.

Get curious. As blogger and public-relations consultant Steve Rubel says, "The most important tool you can have today in business is insatiable curiosity. The minute you lose it, you're dead."[36]

So become curious about your prospective employer. Focus on one organization. What's going on there? What does their annual report tell you about them — their financial results such as the income statement, the balance sheet, and the cash flow? What is their marketplace like? Who are their competitors? What are their products or services? Where are they in the product life cycle? What threats do they face? What chronic problems do they struggle with? What new challenges or opportunities are they encountering? What major initiatives

> We all have a customer, and that customer has problems that need solving.

are they launching? What do you think keeps the CEO awake at night?

What's the Problem?

To begin with, you must clearly define the need or problem you are driven to solve. Here's the key question:

- What is the job that needs to be done — the job only you can do?

Please don't define this job only in terms of an inward-looking job description. The job that needs to be done is the one your customers need from you — whether those customers are external or internal to your organization. We all have a customer, and that customer has problems that need solving.

"There is no shortage of problems," says career advisor Carol Eikleberry. "Whether your problems are small or large, personal or universal, already defined or still unformulated, the creative search for solutions can be deeply engaging and even joyous."[37]

Because you're going to bring your best talents and passions to the cause, defining the problem is a creative process. It's also a question of conscience: what is the problem you ought to solve? "Creativity begins not with problem solving, but with 'problem finding'—with the seeing or sensing of a problem."[38]

Obviously, if you can offer a solution to some critical problem, you've suddenly become very valuable to your employer.

The classic way to define a business problem is to identify the gap between current reality and some desired outcome. If you can put meaningful numbers to the outcome, your solution becomes far more meaningful.

- What is the size of the problem? What is the measurable impact in terms of money, quality of product or service, or customer relationships? Can you express the gap in terms of "X to Y"?

- What is the timing of the problem? Does it occur every day? month? hour? How long would it take to solve? By when could you show progress? Express the timing in terms of "From X to Y by When?"

For example, if you're a Web marketer looking for a job, you could propose increasing traffic to your employer's website, but it's more intriguing and relevant if you can talk about a tenfold increase over a year's time. The centerpiece of your presentation is this: "We can take traffic from X to Y within one year."

Or if you're a finance professional, talk to your prospective employers about speeding up collections 20 percent over the next three quarters and show them the bottomline impact. Again, the centerpiece of your presentation is: "We can decrease collection time from X to Y within three quarters."

The "From X to Y by When" formula is very persuasive.

If you can make a persuasive business case about a problem your prospects care about, they are much more likely to hire you than if you were to simply send them a résumé with the standard cover letter.

In the Knowledge Age, curiosity and research ability are premium if you're going to get the job you want. For instance, a young graduate student named Susan Athey had the gift of driving curiosity. She became the most sought-after job candidate in the American university system some years ago after doing some surprising research. Her story is useful here.

One major problem companies have is getting the right price for their products, and at the same time, paying the right price for supplies. If you get your revenues and expenses out of balance, you can quickly go out of business. Susan was deeply curious about how people decided what prices to charge for things and what prices to pay. It was a simple question about a very complicated subject.

> In the Knowledge Age, curiosity and research ability are premium if you're going to get the job you want.

It started when Susan was a girl in Maryland and her grandfather took her to a cattle auction to buy livestock for his farm. Fascinated, she wondered why cattle were bought and sold in this way. It seemed like an exciting game to her. Sometimes the winners bid more than they should, and everyone had a good laugh at their expense. Sometimes a winner got an amazing deal, so there was a lot of celebration. Susan's curiosity led to graduate research on this question: How can a businessperson make an intelligent investment decision in an uncertain world?

Eventually, Susan Athey became chief economist for Microsoft and a Harvard Business School professor, all because she focused on a question critical to business success and then researched it until she found a unique set of answers. She came up with a better way to analyze risky business decisions and arrive at a solution that diminishes the uncertainty. For this discovery, Susan won the Clark Medal, one of the top awards in the field of economics.

So you might not win the Clark Medal, but you *can* do exactly what Susan did—become an expert on a problem you are interested in and that matters to your employers. *The New York Times* said, "Susan Athey is smart. No surprise there. But by most accounts she's no smarter than others on the market this year. So a look at her other *attributes*, and the kinds of *decisions* she has made to reach this level of success, says a lot about what it takes for a young scholar—or a fledgling athlete, scientist, or entrepreneur, for that matter—to succeed."

What attributes are they talking about? What decisions did Susan make that others neglect to make?

A key attribute is excitement about the problem. "Ms. Athey exudes an enormous pleasure in her research. It is a passion that takes her beyond articulating a problem, into the search for an answer. Ms. Athey thought she'd solved the problem…but there was one loose end: she had not fully described the mathematical structure of her new method, limiting its applicability. Dealing with it involved learning a whole new kind of math. One economist told her 'there was no way I could learn this stuff.…' [She] chose not to follow that advice. When she went home for Christmas, she says, 'I went straight to the library. My dad helped me. We pulled out articles. He Xeroxed them. Then on Christmas night I saw it. Everybody was sleeping. I said, 'I got it, I got it.'"[39]

Now, you don't have to spend your holidays doing research — unless, like Susan Athey, you're so fascinated, you don't want to do anything else. But you do need some of Susan's passion for the problem you're researching. It has to take on some of the feeling of a cause.

About the problem of uncertainty in business decisions, Susan built up a great deal of knowledge capital — the most valuable resource you can have in the Knowledge Age.

So how do you build up your own knowledge capital? How do you do this focused research in order to deeply understand the issues facing your organization?

The Internet is filled with vast resources for understanding a company — its challenges and opportunities and threats. Even a few years ago, this information was hard to get and buried in libraries or periodicals or company archives. Now, with a few clicks, you can

> You do need passion for the problem you're researching. It has to take on some of the feeling of a cause.

learn all about their industry, their financials, their history, their product reviews, their customers—those who love them and hate them—even their leaders and their life stories.

Of course, you still have all the traditional resources as well. Read the periodicals and the industry newsletters.

From Jennifer:

I coach everyone from mid-level managers to executives wanting to become more promotable. The first question I ask them is "What do you read?" If they default to *US Weekly* (which I like, but only after reading the *Harvard Business Review*), then I know we're in trouble.

Then I ask, "Who can you talk to? Find out what they're dealing with and what they're trying to accomplish."

Use the phone or email and find someone in the company who might be willing to spend a few minutes with you. Talk to their customers and suppliers to get a better understanding. What delights the customers? What frustrates them? What do vendors say about the company? Talk to the local sales representative of the company. Why do people buy from the company? Why don't they? Between the Internet and networking, you can piece together a picture of what would be of specific value to them.

From there, you will know if your strengths match up to what they need. Now you can creatively position yourself as a solution, thus differentiating yourself from every other job applicant out there.

Make a Need-Opportunity Presentation

After you've paid the price to understand the challenges the company faces, present yourself as a solution to their problems, not as just another job seeker.

Do *not* go just for a job interview. Go instead for a *Need-Opportunity presentation*.

Describe the need they have and how you can help them meet it. Show a better understanding of their significant issue than the people they already employ. Explain the opportunity you bring to them to meet that need. Show them what life would be like with you and without you. Suggest a trial period — even at your own expense if you have to — until they're convinced that you really are an answer they've desperately needed.

In such an interview, they will learn a few things about you. They will learn that you are a leader. You take initiative to make good things happen. You don't wait to be told what needs to be done — you already know.

For example, a friend tells us about his daughter, who had a degree in marketing and wanted very much to work for a fast-growing new company that made personal-care products. But there were no openings.

So instead of applying for a job, she *created* one. In researching the company, she found they had a chronic problem keeping stores stocked with their shampoos, soaps, and lotions. The out-of-stock problem was a major threat to their relationships with their clients — she knew this because she had talked to the retailers who carried the products.

Then she built a Need-Opportunity presentation and asked for 20 minutes of their time to present it. Essentially, she overviewed the need, demonstrating that she knew a lot about it. She reminded them how much the out-of-stock problem was costing them. Then she proposed that the company hire her to coach retail stores on how to improve their forecasting and ordering processes, which she thought were responsible for the problem. This 20-minute presentation clinched the job.

Here's the outline of her Need-Opportunity presentation:

- Out-of-stocks costing you...
  - You're losing $1.55 per customer in your distributor stores because of out-of-stocks.
  - Up to 9% of customers won't buy again.
- Better forecasting and ordering solves 80% of the problem...
  - Food Network went from 14.7% out-of-stocks to 3.9% in 4 mos., est. increased revenue $437K.
  - Pills Inc. went from 12% to 3% in 6 mos.
- How I improve forecasting/ordering systems...
  - Use continuous rolling forecast method instead of year-by-year.
  - Forecast not only for the category, but at SKU level.

The goal of your Need-Opportunity presentation is to start a conversation. You're no longer just an applicant for a job — you're a potential solution to an important problem. Keep the conversation going. Send a thank-you note after the interview and attach an article or a website for further reading. Invite the prospect into your blog and social media sites (if they're safe!). Make him or her a member of your online "village."

One caution: You must go about all of this in a very principled way. Don't exaggerate anything for effect; don't pad your résumé. Stay very focused on their needs and what you can realistically bring to those needs. Pay the price to know your facts cold. If you take such an approach with decision makers, you will get their attention and blow them away with the depth of your preparation and discipline.

Another caution: Don't come across as a threat. You might look presumptuous to people if you march into their offices, publicly air their problems in front of them, and position yourself as the solution they've always needed. There's a right way to do this and a wrong way. There's a helpful tone of voice and an arrogant tone of voice, and you need to know the difference.

> Pay the price to know your facts cold. If you take such an approach with decision makers, you will get their attention and blow them away with the depth of your preparation and discipline.

From Jennifer:

At one organization I worked for, we had an intern who spent the entire internship making sure we knew how out of touch and ineffective we were, often without presenting any solutions. We didn't extend an offer after graduation.

The right way is to express interest in what they're do-ing and offer to help: "In researching the company, I've learned about the need to keep your high-value prod-ucts in stock. I've been working on a possible way to raise in-stock numbers by making a few adjustments to the forecasting and ordering processes..." This is a help-ful voice, not a self-important voice.

The Need-Opportunity presentation is essential for get-ting the job you want. And if you want to upgrade the job you have, these same guidelines apply. Prepare a Need-Opportunity presentation for your boss. At the end of this chapter, you'll find a tool that will guide you in discover-ing your cause and preparing your presentation.

It Never Ends

You can be sure of one thing in business: the problems don't stop coming. In a way, that very fact is the key to your relevance. You make yourself indispensable and secure your future by being the problem solver your em-ployer can't do without.

Regardless of the job you have, whether you're the CEO or a fast-food fry cook, you can bring your own unique solutions to the everyday problems in front of you. Ask yourself, "How will this job be different because *I am the one doing it?*"

- Suppose you're managing a restaurant that's not known for great customer service. You might ask yourself, "What can I do to surprise and delight the next customer?"

- Suppose you're the director of guest relations for a hotel having trouble attracting guests to return.

Ask yourself, "What can I do today that's new and different to make the guest happier and want to come back?"

- Suppose you work on your company's IT help desk, and there are chronic problems with network speed. Ask yourself, "What can I do to make this computer network faster and more efficient?"

The problems right in front of you might be your greatest opportunities for making the contribution you alone can make. And there are new problems and challenges every day—sometimes every hour. This means you become a knowledge worker, no matter what your job is, because you're bringing your creative mind to bear on real problems on a daily basis.

> The job market doesn't really matter to you. Whether it's good or bad makes no difference.

That's why the job market doesn't really matter to you. Whether it's good or bad makes no difference. If employers see you as a compelling solution to the problems they face, they will value you, regardless of the job market. But you must have the mindset of a problem solver, continually fascinated by new challenges. As we noted at the beginning of the book, if you solve one problem and then rest on your laurels posting photos on Facebook all day, you won't have a great career. As Hermann Hesse said, "Whether you and I and a few others will renew the world someday remains to be seen, but within ourselves we must renew it each day."

"Discover Your Cause" Tool

Fill in these boxes to discover the cause you want to serve in your career or in your current role:

---

1. **The company/industry you are interested in:**

---

2. **The key problem(s) they face:**

    a. Size of the problem (in costs, quality, or relationships)

    b. Timing (the time frame of the problem)

---

3. **The solution you will propose:**

Need-Opportunity Presentation Planner

Fill in these boxes to outline a presentation to give to your prospective employer. Where possible, use charts to illustrate the impact of the need and the opportunity you represent.

Describe the employer's need area:

- Size/timing of problem or opportunity.

Describe how you've contributed to resolving this need in the past:

- Where? What was the impact in numbers?

(Describe projects you've done or educational experiences you've had.)

Describe how you would contribute to resolving this need area for your prospect:

- What is the size/timing of the benefit you bring?
- What methods, tools, or resources would you require?

Teach to Learn

The best way to learn from this book is to teach the content to someone else. Everybody knows that the teacher learns far more than the student. So find someone — a co-worker, a friend, a family member — and teach him or her the insights you've gained. Ask the provocative questions here or come up with your own.

- When were you clearly a solution to a problem your employer had? Tell the story.

- A key suggestion in this book is to "become a volunteer, not an employee." Explain what this means.

- In what ways might you be more of a problem than a solution to your employer? How could you reverse that?

- What goes into preparing a Need-Opportunity presentation? Why is this presentation more likely than the standard employment interview to get you the job you want?

- How is your job different because you are the one doing it?

Contribute Your Best

If you know your strengths and have discovered your cause, you're just about ready to write your Contribution Statement. Remember, this statement will provide the direction for everything you do in your current job, or even for your entire professional life.

Before you write your Contribution Statement, let's deal with a common and understandable feeling you might have.

You might not think you have much to contribute.

It could be you've tried to get job after job and have been turned down. Maybe you don't feel valued at work, or believe you're too young or too old or too unimportant to contribute anything. You might feel alienated or frustrated or obstructed on your career path.

Frankly, many of these feelings come from *your* view of yourself, not from the views of others. If you have a Job Seeker paradigm, you see yourself as a prepackaged product that you're trying to push on a buyer. Your résumé is your product brochure. On the other hand, if you have a Contributor paradigm, you see yourself as a solution to a genuine problem, concern, or opportunity. You have a proposal that will make a difference.

Job Seeker Paradigm	Contributor Paradigm
"I'm a product."	"I'm a solution."
"Because I need a job, will you please hire me?"	"Because you have a significant need, I want to offer you strengths that match that need."
"Here is my résumé."	"Here is my proposal to help you."

The difference between the Job Seeker paradigm and the Contributor paradigm is fundamental. It's the difference between pushing a product and providing a welcome solution. Your main challenge is to change your paradigm of yourself from helpless job seeker to powerful contributor.

I want you to imagine you are at the helm of a huge ship moving forward at high speed. You're the driver. You control the direction of this ship. Now, how is it possible for a single, small person to change the course of something so massive?

To change the ship's course, you move a steering wheel that operates a rudder, which then turns the ship. But the rudder itself can be enormous, perhaps even ten stories tall on some ocean liners.

So what moves the rudder?

A tiny second rudder called a trim tab, which is attached to the big rudder.

Become a Trim Tab

Through the marvels of engineering, when the trim tab swings to one side, it creates just enough vacuum to pull the big rudder around. The trim tab is tiny compared to the size and weight of the ship, yet the trim tab determines the ship's course.

Now, how can your small contribution have any impact on the organization?

Because of the principle of the trim tab.

Far too many people are disengaged from their work; they are neither fulfilled nor excited. Most of all, they feel powerless to change anything, and they blame it on the organization or their boss or their lack of authority or that "nobody's hiring." In truth, you are the creative force of your own job and life. No matter what role you play or where you are, your contribution can make a difference. You can become a trim tab. How? Simply by focusing on what you *can* do—even if it's outside of your job description—and making the small adjustments and improvements that you can contribute.

Listen to the story of Madeline Cartwright, a former teachers' union organizer who became principal of a troubled inner-city school. Her first day there, she found a desperate situation: a filthy building, a discouraged staff, apathetic parents, and children who were just trying to survive in a neighborhood trashed and blighted by the drug culture.

> You are the creative force of your own job and life. No matter what role you play or where you are, your contribution can make a difference.

Madeline had many reasons to be discouraged. What contribution could she possibly make here, where many children were caring for crack-addicted parents, where they weren't sure they could even survive from day to day in this crime-infested nightmare—in a place where school was least on a long list of worries no child should have to face?

Well, one of the first things she did as principal was to get down on her own hands and knees and scrub the overwhelming stench out of the children's lavatory floor.

This simple action produced a surprising result. Word spread quickly about the new principal's action, even into the neighborhood. Madeline had sent a strong signal that things were about to change.

"When I came in, this place was as black as soot," she says. The message to the children was "You're not worth a coat of paint." Recruiting a few parents, she organized a complete cleaning and repainting of the scarred-up old school building until it was a well-scrubbed island of safety.[40]

Cleaning the school was only a first step. Many of the children came to school in the same dirty clothes day after day. Few had pajamas, so they slept in their clothes, often alongside younger children who wet the bed. The dirt and smell embarrassed the students, so Madeline collected spare clothes and organized a raffle to raise $600 for a washing machine and dryer. Children with dirty clothes could change into the extra clothes and go to class. Teachers and other volunteers would wash the clothes, and when the children came back in the afternoon, their own clothes were clean and folded. "This is one of the things you can do to bring about a change," she says. "My kids look good."

Of course, Madeline had critics. It wasn't her job to wash clothes, she was told. Her response?

"Don't tell me what I can't do. I can do something if I want to.... I have a problem, and I have a solution. I am going to put this child's clothes in the washing machine and give him some clean clothes to put on. I can do that."

Madeline knew that clean, comfortable children in a clean, welcoming environment could learn. And her determination spread to others. Soon many were involved in the school. A culture of "doing what it takes" emerged among the faculty and students and their parents. Three years

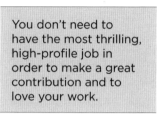

You don't need to have the most thrilling, high-profile job in order to make a great contribution and to love your work.

after Madeline became principal, her school was named the district's most academically improved school.

Madeline Cartwright is a trim tab. What she has contributed is not earthshaking. It did not require strategic planning, great expenditures, or the combined wisdom of presidents and CEOs. Her contribution — cleaning, painting, washing laundry, caring for little children — is perhaps inconsequential in some people's eyes. But the impact — for the people she served and the cause she cared about — is immense. Like Madeline Cartwright, you can become a trim tab by identifying a need and then doing something about it.

You don't need to have the most thrilling, high-profile job in order to make a great contribution and to love your work. Oliver Wendell Holmes said, "Every calling is great when greatly pursued." Each day, you are faced with moments of choice—moments where you can choose to be a trim tab, to go beyond your job description and have tremendous impact right where you are.

Become a trim tab. No matter where you are in the hierarchy of life, no matter where you are in seniority—the youngest new hire or the oldest hand at the helm—you can still make a valuable contribution. It's a great way to work and a more fulfilling way to live.

Now we invite you to write your Contribution Statement. You might want to follow along on your computer or a piece of paper and write as we talk you through the steps. There's also a shorter version of these steps in the "Contribution Statement Builder" tool at the end of the chapter.

Write Your Contribution Statement

Your Contribution Statement is similar to a life mission statement, except that a Contribution Statement defines the high purpose you want to serve and what you intend to achieve in your career or in your current role.

Examples help, so let's imagine what the Contribution Statements of some of these great contributors might have been:

- *"I will provide a clean and safe school, a sanctuary for young children from their harsh environment, where they can learn and grow in comfort and security."* This might have been Madeline Cartwright's Contribution Statement.

- *"I will do the mathematical work that will enable computers to communicate with one another."* This might have been the Contribution Statement of Radia Perlman, the young mathematician who wrote the networking protocols that made the Internet possible.

- *"I will help drug addicts find meaning in their lives beyond drug abuse."* This might have been the Contribution Statement of social worker and minister Hans Visser, who started the popular Via Kunst project in Rotterdam for homeless addicts to work at their own creative projects.[41]

- *"I will help the grieving families of crime victims by finding closure for them."* This might have been the Contribution Statement of Officer Michael Nilles of the Aurora, Illinois, Police, who has resolved several cold cases, including a decade-long mystery about the death of a six-year-old boy.[42]

Each of these ordinary people simply decided what his or her contribution was going to be. None of these things were necessarily in their job descriptions.

You can write a career Contribution Statement. This statement is your "personal value proposition," a summary of your strengths and your commitment to a cause that transcends any particular job.

You can also write a Contribution Statement for your current role at work.

Now, here is the process for writing your Contribution Statement. Spend the time to give this statement your best thinking and quality research. It will pay you back a hundredfold.

1. Write a Tribute to an Influential Person

First, think about the most effective, influential people you have ever known personally. Choose one of them and write a tribute to that person. It could be a teacher, a co-worker, a friend, or a leader you have worked for. What contribution did that person make to your life?

Writing this tribute to another person will help you crystallize in your own mind the kind of contribution you might make in your role.

From Stephen:

Let me give you an example. When I was a very young man, I did some volunteer work abroad. One day my supervisor called me in and assigned me to go around the country and provide training to people who were much more senior than I was. I was shocked and nervous, but he said, "You can do this. I have confidence in you."

What was this man's contribution to my life? He started me on the career I've had ever since—teaching effectiveness and leadership to people across the globe. His contribution was to create other leaders by giving them the confidence and the opportunities to lead.

From Jennifer:

When I was 19 years old, I worked at a department store, attended school full time pursuing my under-graduate degree, and did what college kids do with any remaining time (anything but sleep). But I felt I wasn't doing anything important—anything to make a difference. One day, I heard that the community service center on campus was running Saturday-morning service projects, so I signed up and early Saturday morning went to work at a residential facility for the homeless.

It seemed like all the other students were there with friends, and I didn't know anyone. As I cleaned the floor, I wondered if I had done the right thing coming. Then a woman came up to me and said, "Hi, I'm Irene. I'm the director of the service center. I'm so glad you came today." She made me feel welcome and talked to me about the difference I was making by cleaning the floor. So I signed up for the next monthly project. At that project, she asked me to drop by the center to talk about more volunteer opportunities.

Over the next two years, Irene encouraged me to start an environmentally focused service group (my passion). In my last year of college, she made me the research-and-development director of the center, nominated me as a student representative to the local United Way board, and co-taught with me a college class on community leadership in action. Each time, I was afraid to make the leap; and each time, she encouraged me to take on a new challenge. Irene inspired a lifelong passion for service and an enduring belief in myself that I can overcome my fears and take the next step in my life.

2. Write Tributes You Would Like to Receive

Once you have written your tribute to another person, write down the tributes you would like to receive from other key people in your work — your boss, your fellow team members, your customers.

Someday you will leave the job you are in now. What will you want these people to say about you? How will you want them to remember you? How will they describe the contribution you made in your role?

As you write these tributes, you will find that you can more clearly envision the kind of contribution you could make.

3. Review Your Strengths

Go back to the "Know Your Strengths" tool in this book. Review it carefully.

- What unique knowledge, talents, or skills do you have that can help you make a contribution?

- What job-related opportunities are you passionate about?

- What is your real responsibility to your organization, your customers, and your co-workers?

4. Review Your Cause

Go back to the "Discover Your Cause" tool in this book. Review it carefully.

- What company or industry are you interested in (or already employed in)?

- What key problem(s) do they face?

- What is the size of the problem in costs, quality, or relationships?

- What is the timing of this problem?

- What solution will you propose?

5. Draft Your Contribution Statement

Taking all of this input into consideration, draft your Contribution Statement. At this point, it is only a draft. Too many people are frozen, inactive, waiting for their "calling," their "best life," or their dream career to hit them over the head like a religious conversion. Until then, they remain vaguely dissatisfied with the world and themselves. Don't say, "I'll write it later." Write it now. Write freely. Take your time. You can always go back and rethink, refine, and reshape your statement.

Although a Contribution Statement is personal and can take any form, it might be helpful to follow this format:

> Because *[this problem exists in this organization or industry]*,
> I will use my strengths in *[list your strengths]*
> To *[provide this solution]*.

Here are several examples of this kind of Contribution Statement:

Nurse/Caregiver

Because my aging patients are often irritable and depressed,

I will rely on my calm personality and natural affection for them, along with my training in anger management

To ease their suffering and help them improve their relationships with their loved ones.

Mobile Phone App Developer

Because there is a shortage of high-quality apps for mobile phones (there's a lot of rubbish out there),

I will use my software-design capability in connection with an intuition for what people really want and need

To create a new generation of apps that will truly make life better instead of more cluttered.

Symphony Orchestra Marketing Manager
Because audiences are shrinking and fewer young people are interested in classical music,

I will use my training as a publicist and violinist, along with my passion for growing new, young talent,

To bring the delights of classical music to schools across our community and create a new audience for our orchestra.

Public Utility Operations Director
Because water loss through waste and evaporation is alarmingly high in our city system,

I will leverage my ability to bring people together to solve problems; and with my unique education in both engineering and finance,

I can help everyone arrive at a win-win plan for minimizing this costly drain.

High School Teacher
Because my high-risk students are likely to drop out of school,

I will call on my background as an actor

To make my classes as entertaining as possible in order to hold their interest.

Project Manager
Most software projects fail because of constantly shifting expectations,

focused on producing solid value. The objective is all about the applicant. The Contribution Statement is about how the applicant can help you. Which would you hire?

Now, if you already have a job, can you see the power of writing a Contribution Statement for your current role? If you want to make a more meaningful contribution, make an appointment with your supervisor to share a draft of your statement. Ask for his or her input, and listen. Your supervisor will have a valuable perspective on your statement.

From Jennifer:

Once I walked into the office of a colleague of mine for a meeting. He was smiling and shaking his head. I asked him what was so funny. He said, "I just met with Alison about her desired contribution for the year. It had nothing to do with what my team needs or what the organization needs." He paused "She had some really great ideas—if she were in a totally different organization with a totally different market."

So plan *together* how you can make your contribution.

Share your Contribution Statement with your team members. Let them help you write it. They might even want to write one for themselves.

Peter Drucker says this about sharing your Contribution Statement with your supervisor and your team:

"[Don't] be afraid of being thought presumptuous.... Whenever anyone goes to his or her associates and says, 'This is what I am good at. This is how I work. These are my values. This is the contribution I plan to concentrate on and the results I should be expected to deliver,' the response is always, 'This is most helpful. Why didn't you tell me earlier?'"[43]

Contribution Statement Builder

Follow these steps to write your Contribution Statement:

1. Write a tribute to an influential person.

Think about the most effective, influential people you have ever known personally. Choose one of them and write a tribute to that person. It could be a teacher, a co-worker, a friend, or a leader you have worked for. What contribution did that person make to your life?

2. Write tributes you would like to receive.

Once you have written your tribute to another person, write down the tributes you would like to receive from other key people in your work — your boss, your fellow team members, your customers. Draw on these tributes as you draft your statement.

3. Review your strengths.

Go back to the "Know Your Strengths" tool in this book. Review it carefully.

- What unique knowledge, talents, or skills do you have that can help you make a contribution?
- What job-related opportunities are you passionate about?
- What is your real responsibility to your organization, your customers, and your co-workers?

4. Review your cause.

Go back to the "Discover Your Cause" tool on page 47. Review it carefully.

- What company or industry are you interested in (or already employed in)?
- What key problem(s) do they face?
- What is the size of the problem in costs, quality, or relationships?
- What is the timing of this problem?
- What solution will you propose?

5. Draft your Contribution Statement.

Taking all of this input into consideration, draft your Contribution Statement. Write freely. Take your time. You can always go back and rethink, refine, and reshape your statement.

6. Share your Contribution Statement.

If you're applying for a job, share your statement with the interviewers. Make it the centerpiece of your Need-Opportunity presentation.

If you want to upgrade or transform your job, share your statement with your supervisor. Make an appointment to discuss it in depth. Listen to your supervisor's input. Make a plan together to enable you to make your contribution.

Teach to Learn

The best way to learn from this book is to teach the content to someone else. Everybody knows that the teacher learns far more than the student. So find someone — a co-worker, a friend, a family member — and teach him or her the insights you've gained. Ask the provocative questions here or come up with your own.

- A trim tab is a tiny rudder that influences the direction of a great ship. In what ways could you be a "trim tab" at work and make a significant contribution?

- What tributes would you give to the "trim tab" people in your life? at work?

- If you're looking for a job, what tributes would you like to receive from your prospective employers, co-workers, and customers?

- When you leave your current job, what tributes would you like to receive from your boss? your co-workers? your customers?

- If you want to receive these tributes, what do you have to change now about the way you approach your job? your career?

- Why should you write a Contribution Statement when you're looking for a job? Why should you write a Contribution Statement for your current job?

- What are the steps in writing a Contribution Statement? Explain each step.

- What is the value of sharing your Contribution Statement with your supervisor and your co-workers?

- When and how will you share your Contribution Statement?

PART 2

HOW WILL YOU MAKE YOUR CONTRIBUTION?

Section Overview

- How to get the job you want and overcome obstacles to making your contribution.

- How to build a village—a network of supporters, both co-workers and clients—who can help you achieve your career goals.

- How to write effective résumés and cover letters, succeed in interviews, and give Need-Opportunity presentations.

Get the Job You Want

Now that you've written your Contribution Statement, your task is to make it happen. Only you can do that, but you've got to rise above the traditional Industrial Age mentality if you're going to succeed.

You have to give up being helpless — at the mercy of the economy or your boss or your weak education (or *too much* education), or your skinny résumé or your youth or your age or your gender or your race or your face or your special case.

In other words, you have to give up being a victim. You have to stop blaming your circumstances, trapping yourself in what the great Iranian poet Hafiz called "the sad game":

> *Blame*
> *Keeps the sad game going.*
> *It keeps stealing all your wealth,*
> *Giving it to an imbecile with*
> *No financial skills.*
> *Dear One,*
> *Wise Up.*[44]

It's true: the job market can be a daunting place. Hiring freezes, downsizing, restructuring of whole industries, reductions in force—it all means fewer traditional, secure, well-paying jobs. It also means a lot more competition for many of the best jobs.

At the same time, employers face a host of new challenges in this turbulent era while still grappling with the old problems. To familiar issues like improving sales, product development, and marketing, they add global competition, social responsibility, and online commerce. Ironically, while employers offload employees, they have to hire more and more part-timers, consultants, and contractors. They still must get the work done.

And that's where you come in. No company wants to hire just for the sake of hiring, but they all want to solve problems. They need your contribution like a thirsty man in the desert needs water, but they must first recognize that you *have* water to offer. It's a bit silly to sit in a desert complaining that no one wants the water only you can bring.

Be Strong in the Hard Moments

There are certain hard moments that, if we are strong, will make all the difference in our lives. Hard moments are conflicts between doing what leads to success and just giving up. They are the key tests, the defining moments of life—and how we handle them can literally shape the future. Losing a job is one of those hard moments.

> No company wants to hire just for the sake of hiring, but they all want to solve problems.

When you've been laid off, you can slip quickly into discouragement. It might become harder to get up every day to do your job search. If you're weak in a hard moment and sleep in instead of getting up, it becomes the first of many little failures. If you can conquer yourself and stay strong in these moments, you start accumulating successes. It's so hard to face yet another rejection, but in that hard moment, you keep going. Eventually, you can very likely get or invent the job you want—even if they're "not hiring."

If you feel discouraged, you might be seeing yourself as dependent on others or your circumstances. You see yourself as the product of everything that happens to you. You're not valued at work, your boss has it in

> If you're weak in a hard moment and sleep in instead of getting up, it becomes the first of many little failures.

for you, school never helped you, the world is against you—you're a "loser." Everything depends on luck.

On the other hand, if you have a paradigm of independence, you see yourself as the product of your own choices. Furthermore, you can choose to create your own future. Everything depends on you.

Dependent Paradigm	Independent Paradigm
"I am the product of what happens to me."	"I am the product of my own choices."
"No one wants me."	"I can create my own job."
"I can't change the way I feel about myself."	"I can choose how I feel about myself."

The difference between the dependent paradigm and the independent paradigm is fundamental. It's the difference between letting the future just happen and taking control of it. It's the difference between remaining a slave to your feelings and mastering them. The main challenge is to change your paradigm of yourself from dependent and useless to independent and full of capacity.

The celebrated film director Steven Spielberg is a prime example of the independent paradigm. A teenage movie fanatic when he walked onto the production lot at Universal Studios, he hadn't even graduated from high school. But he wanted a job in film so badly that he just showed up day after day, even though no one wanted him there. It was a lonely feeling. He had no business being on the lot, but he hung around, volunteering for anything that needed to be done.

By doing unpaid odd jobs at the studio, Spielberg got to watch movies being shot and talk to film people and learn the craft of moviemaking. He didn't even have a pass to get into Universal Studios, but as one friend recalled, "Steven found his own way of getting on the lot. Steven was able to walk onto the lot just about any time he pleased."[45] Eventually, the studio invited him to help direct a short film, and he was on his way to a career creating *Jaws, ET, Close Encounters,* the *Indiana Jones* series, and other wildly profitable movies.

On his own initiative, through all the hard moments, Steven Spielberg persisted to become the most financially successful film director in history.[46] On your own initiative, and with the right paradigm, you can knock down virtually any barrier to the career you want.

Work in Your Circle of Influence,
Not Your Circle of Concern

Now, what if nobody answers your phone calls or emails or carefully considered proposals? What if your employers aren't ready to see you in a new or expanded role? What if you're really not in a position to become much of a solution to the problems they care about? What if the obstacles to your success look overwhelming?

If so, you need to work on your Circle of Influence, not your Circle of Concern.

Imagine a circle that contains all the barriers to your career success. This is your Circle of Concern:

Now imagine another, smaller circle inside the Circle of Concern. It contains all the people, knowledge, tools, and capital you have to work with. This is your Circle of Influence. It might be very small for now, but if you invest your energies in growing that Circle of Influence instead of wasting your energies worrying

about your Circle of Concern, your power to build
your career will grow.

A marvelous example of a person who started small
within her Circle of Influence was Dr. Elisabeth Kübler-
Ross, a Swiss psychiatrist who, in the 1950s, began her
career as a lowly intern in a very large hospital. Doing
exhausting rounds as all new doctors do, she was dis-
turbed by the way the hospital staff treated terminally
ill patients. The dying were lied to about their condi-
tion, ignored, and often left to die alone. So she began to
break out of the routine and just sit with patients in the
last stage of life, listening to their stories as they poured
out their hearts to her. And she noticed that they would
feel better, more at peace, after these visits.

Gradually, Dr. Kübler-Ross became more and more knowledgeable about how to treat the spirit of these patients who
could no longer be treated for their physical ailments. Other
doctors asked her to help their patients. Hospital administra-
tors became interested in her work, which was entirely out-

side her job description. Eventually, a publisher approached her, and in 1969 she wrote *On Death and Dying*, a landmark book that transformed how the medical profession deals with patients at the end of life.

By working within her own small Circle of Influence, an intern of no particular importance with no institutional authority expanded that circle to influence the whole world. When she started her career, she had few resources within her Circle of Influence — only her basic medical education and her own talents, passion, and conscience. But she sensed a vast need and began to leverage her few resources to fill it.

> Finding the job you want is 90 percent research!

When Steven Spielberg crashed the gate at Universal Studios as a teenager, his Circle of Influence was microscopic. But by building relationships, learning the film-making craft, and mastering the tools of the trade, he expanded his Circle of Influence to encompass a whole industry.

Anyone can do the same. In your Circle of Concern, fill in your most important concerns about your career. In your Circle of Influence, fill in those items you have some influence over, and then start working on them instead of wasting time on the Circle of Concern. You'll be pleased as you become more relevant and more important to your organization.

If you have a Knowledge Age mentality, you'll soon realize that you have abundant resources within your Circle of Influence for solving an employer's key problems. Of course, most people don't make the effort to find those resources. This is where research comes in.

Remember, finding the job you want is 90 percent research!

A few years ago, a young man named Dan was hired as a technical writer for a small credit-card processing company. He did good work, but when tough times came along, his job was threatened, along with the marketing department he worked for. Instead of sitting around like a victim waiting for the inevitable layoff, he took a proactive stance. He looked into why his company was about to downsize him out of a job, and found that there was a serious cash-flow problem. The reason for the problem? In the economic downturn, more and more customers were failing to pay their bills on time.

So Dan went to management and volunteered to help with the cash-flow problem by speeding up collections. Surprised, they accepted his offer to help; took him out of his old, now less relevant job; and gave him a new, very relevant job—to contact delinquent customers and collect payments. He worked very hard to learn the best ways to collect on aging accounts. Soon he was making a real difference to company cash flow.

In this new role, Dan got curious about why so many customers wouldn't pay up and, with a little research, found that a certain number of them had been bad risks from the start. He then got interested in how to avoid the problem instead of just fixing it—in other words, how to keep untrustworthy people from getting credit-card accounts in the first place.

Dan started to see the glimmer of a new and powerful contribution he could make—to protect his company from credit-card fraud.

So he dived into his Circle of Influence. He found on-line communities to join, people to talk to, and seminars to attend. He researched the gaps in his knowledge, the technology and tools he would need, and how to get the budget for these things.

The Circle of Influence below shows Dan's research agenda.

Dan's Circle of Influence

Sources of Knowledge
- Ideas from Fraud textbook
  - "Bill to" different from "Ship to"
  - Orders from free email addresses
  - Big order, next-day delivery
  - International orders
- Global Anti-Fraud seminar, April
- Fraud Prevention Ass'n.

Budget
Need software—campaign for a line item in the quality control budget.

Technology/Tools
- Fraud prevention software
- Pattern detection system
- Database of known fraudsters

People to Talk To
- Jin, CFO
- Julie at ecommercerisk
- Carl at Harper Group
- George@corporateintsec
- Rona, quality-control budget officer

- **People.** He sought out the right people who could help him learn about the problem. He got acquainted with the community of risk managers on the Internet, showering them with questions on their blogs. He talked to the Chief Financial

Officer of his company to get a sense of how big the fraud problem was. He connected with the quality-control office, which had an important role in the security of the company's transactions.

- **Knowledge.** He read deeply on the subject. Books and websites on fraud in the finance industry were a big help. He learned about the telltale signs that a fraudster is at work in Internet commerce. He joined the Fraud Prevention Association and went to their seminars. It became fascinating for him, and he discovered a passion for detective work that he didn't know he had.

- **Technology/Tools.** He became very familiar with the range of software and technological systems available for detecting fraud. He learned how to use cutting-edge tools that can flag potential fraud by analyzing subtle patterns in Web traffic.

- **Budget.** He created a business case for his employers to show them how the fraud problem was hurting them financially, and to request the tools and the training he needed to solve this problem. He clearly laid out the return on their investment.

If you're going to do research effectively, you should think in terms of resource people, sources of knowledge, and technology solutions. Don't forget the budget you'll need to do a good job.

When Dan took his proposal to his employers, they leaped at the chance to stop this hemorrhage from their bottom line. After a lot of experimentation, trial and error, and more probing and study, he made a real difference. He helped his company save tens of thousands of dollars.

> The tougher things get, the more crucial the concerns your employer faces; and the more solution-oriented you become, the more valuable you are.

If all this sounds like a lot of work, you're right. But it's worth it. This kind of work separates a merely good career from a great one. Of course, in Dan's case, it made the difference between having a great job and having no job at all. As his Circle of Influence grew, his responsibilities and satisfactions grew as well.

Eventually, Dan went on to a new, more responsible job with a much bigger company. Within the first few weeks, his work led to the capture of a clever fraudster who had stolen more than a quarter of a million dollars from his new employer. Dan became a recognized authority in the detection and prevention of credit-card fraud.

Dan went from employee to volunteer. He went from reactively answering a low-level job description to proactively solving a serious business problem. In a job he invented for himself, he is now virtually indispensable to the company he works for.

When you think about it, Dan did what anyone can do. Tough times gave Dan the opportunity he needed. You can find and capitalize on the same kinds of opportunities. The tougher things get, the more crucial the concerns your employer faces; the more solution-oriented you become, the more valuable you are.

Believe us—if you can help your employer win, your chances of winning go way up.

At the end of this chapter, there is a "Circle of Influence" tool to help you do what Dan did. You'll be surprised how many resources you actually have that can help you get or keep the job you want.

Now, suppose Dan had decided to focus on his Circle of Concern instead of his Circle of Influence? What might he have written into his Circle of Concern?

Dan's Circle of Concern

- My technical-writing job is no longer needed.
- My department is being eliminated.
- The economy is bad.
- The company's cash flow is slowing down—what can I do about it?
- My supervisors don't see beyond my job description.
- I don't have the training to work with customers.

Dan could have sat back passively, like a victim, and blamed the impending loss of his job on these very real things he had little or no control over. After all, these obstacles were not illusions! But he took a proactive approach and refused to play the victim.

Your goal is to grow your Circle of Influence. You do that by focusing your best energies on those things you can influence. Over time, you become more and more influential, the Circle of Influence gets bigger and bigger, and the Circle of Concern takes care of itself.

Dan worked on his Circle of Influence. He found out how to improve cash flow. He educated himself on customer issues. He learned the best practices for collecting on late accounts. And his employers learned to value him far beyond his old job.

You can start the way Dan did—by working on those things you can do something about. That start can be very small and perhaps, at first, unnoticed by your employer. The "Circle of Influence" tool on the next page can help you focus on the things you can do something about.

"Circle of Influence" Tool

This tool will help you overcome the barriers to getting the job and career you want. You might want to fill in several of these circles.

1. Write into the Circle of Concern the most important barriers to making your career contribution happen. Number them.

2. Insert into the Circle of Influence the numbers of those items you have some influence over.

   - Who would be willing to help you?

   - What are your key sources of knowledge — books, periodicals, blogs, Internet newsletters, and so forth?

   - What technology and tools can help you solve the problem?

   - Where can you qualify for budget, if necessary?

3. Make a plan to act on those items in your Circle of Influence, and watch the circle grow!

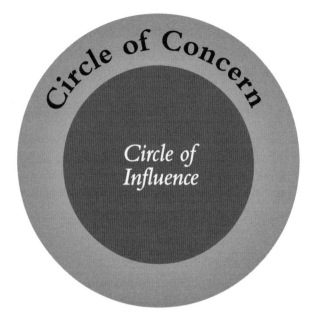

Actions I will take to increase my Circle of Influence:

1. _____

_____

2. _____

_____

3. _____

_____

4. _____

_____

Teach to Learn

The best way to learn from this book is to teach the content to someone else. Everybody knows that the teacher learns far more than the student. So find someone — a co-worker, a friend, a family member — and teach him or her the insights you've gained. Ask the provocative questions here or come up with your own.

- Why is the "victim mentality" so crippling to people who are trying to create a great career?

- Why is it so important to adopt a proactive mentality about your career?

- Do you talk like a victim? Do you find yourself blaming other people or your circumstances for your lack of career progress? How could you change your language to reflect a more proactive mentality?

- Can you think of instances where you've used your own initiative to make an important contribution at work?

- "Getting the job you want is 90 percent research." Explain why this is true.

- Why do people so often underestimate the resources available to them in finding the job they want?

- What does it mean to "act in your Circle of Influence rather than your Circle of Concern" in finding the job you want?

Build Your Own Village

Now, there's another key principle to live by if you want a great job and a great career. We call it "building your own village." By that we mean creating and maintaining authentic relationships with key people who mutually support each other. They help you in building your great career, and you in turn contribute to their success. Your career success depends not only on yourself, but also on the people around you. In the workplace, you never achieve anything worthwhile alone.

One of the most common bits of advice for the job seeker is to "network."

In some respects, networking is a relic of the Industrial Age. Too often, networking comes down to having a lot of contacts on your iPhone or BlackBerry—a big list of names you will never know what to do with. Or you have a drawer full of business cards from people you can't even place any more.

Industrial Age thinking sees people as tools. People are tempted to see each other as "means to an end." They seek out others only when they need something from them, as you might go to a toolbox for a hammer or a pair of scissors when you need it. It's hard to have a genuine, authentic, loving relationship with a pair of scissors.

Industrial Age Paradigm	Knowledge Age Paradigm
"Other people are tools—means to an end."	"Other people are important to me in themselves."
"I seek people out when I need something from them."	"I seek people out to strengthen my relationship with them."
"I have a large network of contacts."	"I belong to a village whose members have strong, authentic ties to one another and who serve one another."

By contrast, in the Knowledge Age, people are not tools. They are important in themselves. In a healthy family or friendship, this has always been true, but not in the Industrial Age workplace. Authentic relationships with co-workers, customers, and suppliers are becoming essential. Intriguingly, a Gallup study has found that one of the top indicators of great performance in the workplace is having a best friend at work.[47]

So network from a Knowledge Age mindset rather than an Industrial Age mindset. The best networkers are building a village of people who value one another for more than just what they can *do* for one another.

From Jennifer:

A couple of years ago, I had the opportunity to interview Jack Welch, the former CEO of GE, at a leadership event in front of several thousand people. The next week, I received a handwritten note from him expressing his pleasure in meeting me and thanking me for the experience. I have no doubt that Jack Welch has an extensive network and didn't need anything from me. He was just doing what he has always done to build connections in his career.

Contribute to the Village

Let us tell you about Luke, who works for one of our client companies. Luke maintains a list of people he keeps close to, not only family and friends, but also in the business. These are co-workers and customers. Through Facebook, he knows when he last made contact and makes sure that every few days or weeks, he connects with them again. When he comes across an article that might interest one of his contacts, he passes it on with a note. If a "villager" has won a big client or earned a promotion, he sends a congratulatory email. He's not a salesman who might call people only to make a sale. He's not a "schmoozer" looking for "useful" contacts. His messages are not irrelevant updates on his life. He makes genuine and frequent contact with these people out of a sincere desire to know them better and serve them better. "I am building my own village," he says.

> Visualize with us the personal atmosphere of the old-time village. People knew each other well — they spent time talking, laughing, and working together.

Most of us live in rather impersonal communities these days, but visualize with us the personal atmosphere of the old-time village. People knew each other well—they spent time talking, laughing, and working together. They ate together. They celebrated together. Their relationships were deep, lasting, and authentic.

Luke selected the term "village" for a powerful reason. His purpose is not to "use" others as levers for his career;

instead, he sees building his village as central to the *definition* of his career.

Hark back to the words *métier*, ministry, or calling. These words meant something. A meaningful career is about meaningful service. Where a village is about mutual affection and support, a network is too often about serving yourself. Where a village is about people, a network is too often about machinery.

We tend to assume that some jobs, like teacher or social worker, are more about service than others. Some professions are even categorized as "service jobs," but this is a misleading paradigm. People with great careers always have a service paradigm. If you believe that what you do truly makes the lives of others better, if you satisfy a real business need or delight a child or inspire the mind, then you are serving others in your work.

When drought hit the tiny village of Masitala, Malawi, the farms suffocated under merciless windstorms of orange dust. The Kamkwamba family, like others in the village, were in a desperate situation as they watched their soybeans and maize dry up into dead sticks. Without water, there could be no future for the village.

At 15, young William Kamkwamba had to quit school because his father could no longer afford the $80 yearly tuition. So William looked around for a solution to the plight of the village. He knew that water could be

> People with great careers always have a service paradigm.

found in deep wells nearby—the problem was pumping the water to the surface. But without electricity, there was no practical way to do it.

Then, in an old library book, William saw a picture of a windmill and started to think about harnessing the dry wind to generate electricity. Barely able to read English, he painstakingly deciphered the technical terms in the book and made a plan.

Without money for materials, he went to a junkyard and salvaged an abandoned tractor rotor to control the windmill propeller. For the tower, he lashed together blue-gum tree trunks and built a generator out of old bicycle parts. His circuit breaker was a pair of nails, a magnet, and coils of copper wire. The family believed William was wasting his time until the generator lit up a light bulb inside the family home. The mill soon powered a pump that irrigated new life into the dying fields.

Over several years, William refined his invention. Now that he has built many more advanced windmills, the 60 families of Masitala enjoy enough electricity to bring water to their farms and to light their houses. William Kamkwamba has a career and a contribution to make: "to power up his country, one windmill at a time."[48] Serving the needs of his village is William's career.

One of the great paradoxes of life is that the self-serving careerist never has a great career. That's because such a person's vision never extends beyond the next rung on the corporate ladder. The careerist is a relic of the Industrial Age, a time when, as Richard Ohmann put it, "procedures supplant[ed] value and people [were] absorbed in structures"[49] and people were willing to do anything to get ahead. By contrast, the vision of a William Kamkwamba is about giving real value to real people. Is there anyone who doubts that William will have a great career?

Some day, someone will sum up your career. Will you be just another link in a giant impersonal network? Or will you be remembered as one who served and contributed and gave your best to the "village"?

How do you build your village? Here are four suggestions: (1) identify the members of your village, (2) create an Emotional Bank Account with each member of your village, (3) carve out your own space on the Internet, and (4) practice synergy.

Identify the Members of Your Village

Who naturally belongs to your village? There are two kinds of people: those you serve and support, and those who serve and support you. Start by listing the half dozen or so people who are most important to your career. They might be a major client, your boss, a key co-worker, an agent, or an old school friend who stimulates you to think creatively.

Identify the roles each person plays in your career. Their titles are less important than what you do for them or what they do for you. What are the real roles of your supervisor? Just plain "boss"? Or mentor? Customer? Reality checker? Coach?

> Some day, someone will sum up your career. Will you be just another link in a giant impersonal network?

What are the real roles of your clients? Are they just sources of revenue? Or can they become valued friends who are rich with information, advice, and contacts?

How many people belong to your village? It depends. If to build your career you need 10,000 followers on Twitter, that's fine. On the other hand, most of us can build truly authentic relationships with only a few people because it takes so much time and energy to do so. Still, a genuine village relationship can pay enormous dividends.

Anyway, most of us don't need a whole city to build a great career—a village will do. You can grow very influential within the sphere of your customers and coworkers. William Kamkwamba didn't need a big playing field to make a big impact.

Create an Emotional Bank Account

Once you've identified the members of your village, create an "Emotional Bank Account" with each one. You know what a financial bank account is. You make deposits into it and build up a reserve from which you can make withdrawals when you need to. An Emotional Bank Account is a metaphor that describes the amount of trust and confidence in a relationship.

If I make deposits into an Emotional Bank Account with you through service, good will, small courtesies, honesty,

> Most of us don't need a whole city to build a great career—a village will do.

and keeping my commitments to you, I build up a reserve. Your confidence in me rises, and you will come to my aid if I need you. I can even make mistakes in our relationship, and that high confidence level, that reserve in the "emotional bank," will compensate for it.

But if I have a habit of ignoring you until I need something from you—of treating you like a tool instead of a person—eventually, I overdraw my Emotional Bank

Account with you. Trust levels drop. Eventually, we deal with each other remotely, at a distance, as tools to serve our own interests rather than building "win-win" relationships with each other.

In the Industrial Age paradigm, people are tools. That's why the Industrial Age workplace is filled with

> Inauthentic relationships are one source of the mindless "busyness" in the workplace.

tension. Outside of work, many families are filled with it. Many marriages are filled with it. If the account doesn't receive continuing deposits, any relationship will deteriorate.

The dreaded, so-often-heard greeting in the workplace is not an authentic "Hello, how are you?" It's "I know you're busy, but…" When people greet you this way, it often means their only interest in you is how you can help them with their emergency. This means that you're a tool to them. Your value is what you can do for them right now. No wonder responding to urgent requests can become your life. Inauthentic relationships are one source of the mindless "busyness" in the workplace.

This doesn't mean you shouldn't help people who really need you. Not at all — quite the reverse. A great career is all about helping people. In fact, a good response to the greeting "I know you're busy, but…" is "I'm never too busy to talk to you."

But that response can only be authentic if you see your career as serving people *within the boundaries of your Contribution Statement*. If you want a great career, you can't respond to every request; otherwise, your career goes off on a million tangents. When you commit yourself to making a great, carefully defined contribution, you also commit yourself to saying no — courteously — to activities that won't help you make your contribution.

> When you plan your time, deliberately schedule activities to build your relationship with the members of your village.

If the request is urgent but outside the limits of your Contribution Statement, you can help find someone else to do it or decline with an honest explanation about your priorities. If you've built a healthy Emotional Bank Account with the person making the request, it won't be a problem.

Now you can see why it is so important to live by your Contribution Statement. Without it as a rudder, you can easily drift off course trying to please everybody. In the end, you'll be everyone's doormat, and you'll never make a substantive contribution of your own.

Here's how to build your Emotional Bank Account with people.

When you plan your time, deliberately schedule activities to build your relationship with the members of your village. You'll have lunch. You'll send a thank-you message. You'll write blog entries celebrating them. You'll set aside time to help with their project. You'll forward an article you read that will help them with their work.

And you'll do these things *regularly* and *frequently*. At the start of every week, ask yourself, "What can I do for this person this week? What deposit can I make in the Emotional Bank Account?" And then follow through. The people in your village might change from time to time, but your habit of making deposits must never change.

Carve Out Space on the Internet

Social media tools are a two-edged sword when it comes to networking. At their best, Facebook, Twitter, and LinkedIn enable you to build your village. At their worst, these tools enable billions of one-sided conversations—a sad, empty sort of reaching out to connect with other human beings who aren't even listening.

> The Internet is like a great city, but you can build your own village within that city.

So use social media to *build* your career, not to waste it. Carve out space for yourself on the Internet so people know to turn to you for expertise in your field. The Internet is like a great city, but you can build your own village within that city.

Above all, you should start a career blog. Whether you already have a job or are looking for a job, a career blog is an easy way to connect with the village you're building. You can set it up quickly and take a few minutes to add to it every day. On your blog, you can publish your career Contribution Statement, which will draw followers who value your contribution. Showcase your generic résumé. Regularly post your ideas, discoveries, readings, and accomplishments related to your contribution. Invite people who share your passion to add their own content. And stick with it—the richness and longevity of your blog can make a huge difference in building a great career.

If you already have a personal blog, create a separate career blog. You don't want your business contacts searching through photos of your cat for your latest blog entry on business.

Your blog can be even more important than a business card when you're looking for a job. A real advantage of a blog is that recruiters and customers will find you because they are looking for help. You don't have to look for them. If you provide answers they desperately need, you'll be getting proposals from them. Plus, you can direct recruiters to your blog, which will be far more useful to them in understanding your strengths than your résumé could ever be. Your blog is a résumé on steroids!

Here is a real example of a blogger who got a job as a result of his blog:

> After my employment ended with my last company, I reached out to my network (both the one I built here locally and the one I built through blogging and other social media). I posted on my blog. I posted on Twitter. So did a ton of other people. I was flattered, humbled, and feeling a little bit egotistical about the attention. What can I say, I am human! The conflicts of emotion were interesting....
>
> Last week, I received a message from someone who wanted to talk about how I could work with their company. They were going to be launching a big-time product upgrade and they were targeting the niche I have been working in for the past six years.... They commented on my blog in January (this is why longevity counts) and saw the overwhelming response after I was back on the market.
>
> We talked by phone and sent emails back and forth (none of those emails or conversations included a résumé or application or formal interview questions). It was truly a conversation. After we ham-

mered out some details, I agreed to start immediately.[50]

Please note that this blogger didn't have to do any of the
traditional things people are used to doing in a job search.
No need for a résumé or an application or interview.
What mattered was the conversation among knowledge
workers.

In addition to a blog, consider writing an e-book. Of
course, one way to become recognized as an authority is to write a book. But publishing a book has been
an expensive and difficult undertaking until recently. E-
books are inexpensive to make and easy to distribute. If
your Contribution Statement is relevant, you could have
a thousand or even a million readers overnight.

A good example is Indian entrepreneur Shyam Go-
karn. Recognizing that wine consumption in India
had been increasing 30 percent per year, Shyam combined his love for wine with a marketing instinct to
produce a 540-page e-book, *Cutting Edge Issues of
Marketing Wine in India*. He has carved out a unique
space on the Internet for anyone interested in the ex-
plosive growth of the Indian wine business. This village is large, energetic, highly specialized, and growing
more lucrative every day.

Former Apple marketer Steve Chazin has published a
popular e-book and blog on Apple's marketing secrets. As
a result, he has many followers who pay him for consulting and speaking engagements. People in his village "get a
sense of who I am from the e-book and the blog in a way
that a résumé can't possibly deliver. There is also a sense of
importance the e-book has that a résumé doesn't."[51]

More and more, your online presence will make the big difference in building your great career. (Of course, the opposite is also true: your career might suffer if you post photos from last Friday night on Facebook or Twitter about your pedicure.)

In the age of social media, you can establish and control your personal brand across the world. It does your career little good to have a unique ability to contribute if no one knows about it beyond those you meet face to face. A very experienced recruiter says this: "All recruiters hire through their networks. They'll say, 'I've kept up with her via email and now LinkedIn since we worked together ten years ago.' Or 'I read his blog.' Or 'I'm hiring him because everyone in the SAP implementation field knows him and what he represents—his e-book demonstrates that.'"

> Establish and control your personal brand across the world. It does your career little good to have a unique ability to contribute if no one knows about it.

As a blogger, you become the ultimate knowledge worker, creating a worldwide conversation on the work you're passionate about. Your online presence enables you to become known in your field and establish a reputation for bringing people together to solve problems. You develop a personal brand that can have global value.

Practice Synergy

The village you build might ultimately be your greatest career achievement. It might even become the source of great new advances in understanding your field.

A one-of-a-kind example is Damian Counsell, a former biological scientist who combines his passion for computers, biology, and photo imagery into a global conversation around wedding photography, of all things. His blog features tips for taking and editing pictures, reviews of new cameras, beautiful galleries of photos, and scientific thought pieces. He even directs people to competitor sites and displays their work. His wedding-photography business seems almost incidental to the extraordinary discussions that go on.[52]

> A highly synergistic team creates solutions that even the lone genius cannot foresee.

Damian's blog illustrates the power of synergy. What is synergy? Simply defined, it means that the whole is greater than the sum of its parts. If you put two pieces of wood together, they will bear much more weight than either piece could separately. With synergy, $1+1=3$ or 100 or 1,000.

The village Damian has built discovers new insights every day into the art and business of photography. For example, a number of people contribute to a discussion on the physics of light when taking a picture, leading to new ideas about using a camera to capture reality. Another discussion explores "slicing" a picture to produce a three-dimensional image. This one blog could advance the art of photography a thousandfold.

And isn't that what a great career is all about: making a great contribution? Such a contribution is hardly ever the work of one lone genius. Because of the natural diversity of minds and the uniqueness of each individual member, a highly synergistic team creates solutions that even the lone genius cannot foresee.

You've probably never heard of the inventor of the Internet because no one in particular can claim that title. The Web truly is the product of synergistic teams working on various problems over the past 50 years. One key person in the development of the Internet was Bob Taylor.

A young psychologist during the 1960s, Bob managed projects for the U.S. Government's Office of Advanced Research and Technology. He was annoyed at being forced to log on to three different computers to do his work and thought how convenient it would be if the computers could talk to each other. Fascinated by the problem, he began to build a village to solve it.

He turned to Larry Roberts, an engineer who had once succeeded in linking a computer on the West Coast to another computer on the East Coast. Installed in the Pentagon, Larry began to work out the protocols for relaying information from one set of computers to another. The idea was to treat a computer like a mail box from which messages could be sent to many different destinations. Doug Engelbart, the inventor of the computer mouse, brought to the village his programming expertise from the Stanford Research Institute at Menlo Park, California. Another villager was Ivan Sutherland, who had figured out how to draw graphics on a computer and wanted to send images over the new network, not just text. He linked up with the group from his lab in Salt Lake City, Utah. Paul Baran of the RAND Corporation had helped invent a system called "packet switching" to preserve electronic communications for America's military in the event of war. And many others moved in and out of the village over a period of years. Then, in 1969, the first email messages were sent between computers.

Baran recalls that the process of creating the Internet was "like building a cathedral...new people come along and each lays down a block on top of the old foundations.... Next month another block is placed atop the previous one...the reality is that each contribution follows onto previous work. Everything is tied to everything else."[53]

> It's a natural principle that you cannot achieve anything truly worthwhile alone—at least not in the world of work.

The Internet was a mirror of the village that people like Bob Taylor built. It was a village that spanned a continent made up of people with many diverse strengths and passions, all acting in synergy with each other. And it was driven by a compelling problem. It's fitting that the Internet will probably become your key tool for creating *your* village.

It's a natural principle that you cannot achieve anything truly worthwhile alone at least not in the world of work. The energy you invest in *regularly* and *frequently* building your village will pay dividends not only in advancing your career, but also in personal satisfaction. You will get into the habit of service, which is the foundation of a great career. With a synergy mindset, you will learn from the best people in your life. And when you need them, they'll be there for you because you have been there for them.

"Build Your Village" Tool

Your great career depends not only on you, but also on the village you build around yourself. In the workplace, you never achieve anything worthwhile alone. To build your village, follow these steps:

1. List the people you know who are key to your career success.

2. Note why they belong in your village. What strengths do they bring that you can leverage?

3. Note something you could do this week to make a deposit in a few Emotional Bank Accounts.

4. Each week, review your list, changing it as needed. Then make your weekly deposit in the Emotional Bank Account.

Sample deposits in the Emotional Bank Account:

- Congratulate the person on a job well done.

- Write a tribute to the person in your blog.

- Email an article that will help the person in his or her work.

- Invite him or her to lunch.

- Offer to help with a project that is important to that person.

- Send birthday greetings.

Teach to Learn

The best way to learn from this book is to teach the content to someone else. Everybody knows that the teacher learns far more than the student. So find someone — a co-worker, a friend, a family member — and teach him or her the insights you've gained. Ask the provocative questions here or come up with your own.

- Why is "building your village" central to the definition of a great career?

- What are some differences between a village and a network?

- What is an Emotional Bank Account? How do you make deposits?

- What is a "careerist"? Why is he or she a "relic of the Industrial Age"? Why can't a careerist ever enjoy a great career?

- Why is a blog or other social medium important to your career? What can you do on your blog to build your career?

- What is synergy? What are the advantages of synergistic relationships with others as you build your career?

Frequently Asked Questions

Q: What does a great résumé look like?

A: The purpose of a résumé — or curriculum vitae (CV) — is to get you an interview with the right person. It's a document that briefly presents your skills, education, and experience. Because it's like a product brochure in which you are the product, it must answer the employer's question: "What can you do for me?"

The days of the self-centered résumé are over. The old-fashioned Industrial Age résumé starts with the applicant's self-serving objective — "A rewarding position in a firm that can make me rich and successful" — and then trumpets the whole story of the applicant's life. The typical applicant sends the résumé to 30 different companies and waits to see if one will bite.

Research the employer before writing your résumé. Study the job announcement or description. Make an outline that shows how your experience and education match up with the job requirements.

Do not send a "one size fits all" résumé. If you already have a résumé, rewrite it to target the specific needs and requirements of the job you're applying for.

Frankly, decision makers today don't have the time or inclination to study your life story and make your dreams come true. They have real problems and opportunities, and they need help with them. Therefore, your résumé needs to address those problems and opportunities spot-on. Your résumé needs to show *specifically* and *quantitatively* how life will be better for them if they bring you on board.

> If you already have a résumé, rewrite it to target the specific needs and requirements of the job you're applying for.

There are two kinds of résumés: generic and targeted. You should have a generic résumé that you can post on your social-media site and hand to prospects as you encounter them.

A targeted résumé is quite different. It's aimed at *one* prospective employer and is the product of serious research into that organization. If you really want that job—the one you've researched, the one you're passionate about—you send them a targeted résumé.

A targeted résumé is tailored carefully to reflect the mission and values of the organization, as well as the specific job description.

Let's look at some samples of both generic and targeted résumés.

Here's a generic one-page résumé of a sales manager named Christiane Creer.

Sample Generic Résumé

CHRISTIANE CREER
cc@domail.ca

133 Yale Road
Northvale, BC V1B 2D3

Telephone/Messages:
(604) 555-3789

SENIOR SALES AND OPERATIONS EXECUTIVE

Sales leader with 10+ years of driving profitable growth through innovative sales and sales operations strategies. Performed as Top National Salesperson for two software-engineering companies.

SKILLS

Strategic Planning	Six Sigma & Analytics	Marketing Research
Strategic Alliances	Relationship Selling	Contract Management
CRM	Direct Marketing	Social Media

PERFORMANCE HIGHLIGHTS

- Boosted leads to 238 from <30 while cutting marketing costs 9%. (AAA Consulting)
- Created, in one year, a proactive marketing program that increased positive media coverage 650%. (AAA Consulting)
- Led cross-functional team that cut costs 50% by implementing preconfigured hosting solutions. (BBB Software)
- Increased the identification-stage pipeline 239% and the qualified-stage pipeline 249% through Portfolio Management program. (SSS Consulting)
- Developed a comprehensive sales/marketing program and built a culture of relationship selling—achieved 140% of the overall revenue plan. (CCC Software)
- Recruited 97 new accounts that delivered net revenue of $120K+ per month. (CCC Software)
- Restructured sales organization to build a high-caliber, market-driven team. Increased annual closing volume from $37.2M to $48.4M within 24 months. (CCC Software)

CAREER TRACK

• Director, Sales Operations, AAA Consulting, Vancouver, BC	2006 – present
• Sales Manager, BBB Software, Toronto, ON	2005 – 2006
• Client Partner, SSS Consulting, Chicago, IL	2001 – 2005
• Business Development Manager, CCC Software, Montréal, QC	1999 – 2001

EDUCATION

- MBA, Purdue University – Krannert School of Management, West Lafayette, IN
- BS, University of Colorado, Boulder, CO – Computer Engineering

These features make this résumé well designed:

- Contact information set off from the text.

- A brief profile with a list of skills. In 10 seconds or less, anyone can quickly grasp what Christiane does.

- A selection of performance highlights—her most important career accomplishments. Note that she uses numbers to give a clear picture of the significance of those accomplishments. Even if you don't have exact numbers, you can estimate.

Not This	This
Increased sales leads and cut marketing costs.	Boosted leads to 238 from less than 30 per week while cutting marketing costs 9%.
Created marketing program to increase positive media coverage.	Created, in one year, a proactive marketing program that increased positive media coverage 650%.
Led cross-functional team that cut website hosting costs.	Led cross-functional team that cut costs 50% by implementing preconfigured website hosting solutions.

- Career and education history starting with the most recent.

- Simple font, attractive headings, uncluttered but complete.

- No references, hobbies, or other personal information. Those things can wait for another time. Include in your résumé only information relevant to the requirements of the job.

Now, let's look at a targeted résumé from Christiane aimed at a particular job: Sales Director for a large computer software company. The job announcement calls for applicants with these qualifications:

- Excellent track record in managing relationship selling, coupled with a broad knowledge of customer-relationship management CRM programs.
- History of successful turnarounds in sales performance.
- Deep background in market research and analytics.

So Christiane tailors her résumé to emphasize her abilities in these areas. She rewrites her profile statement to prioritize her experience in revitalizing sales teams as a "strong proponent of market research." She reorders her accomplishments to prioritize relationship selling, successful turnaround of a sales team, and market research. She adds to the one-page résumé another page describing these achievements in more detail because she knows this information is important to the prospect.

Here's the résumé she sends:

Sample Targeted Résumé

CHRISTIANE CREER
cc@domail.ca

133 Yale Road
Northvale, BC V1B 2D3

Telephone/Messages:
(604) 555-3789

SENIOR SALES AND OPERATIONS EXECUTIVE

Dedicated sales operations and product management leader who revitalizes sales teams. Strong proponent of market research, instilling into the sales group the disciplines of data analysis, creativity, and collaboration. **Top National Salesperson** for two software companies.

SKILLS

Relationship Selling	Marketing Research	Six Sigma & Analytics
CRM	Strategic Planning	Contract Management
Strategic Alliances	Direct Marketing	Social Media

SELECT PERFORMANCE HIGHLIGHTS

- Developed a comprehensive sales/marketing program and built a culture of relationship selling that achieved 140% of the overall revenue plan. (CCC Software)
- Restructured sales organization to build a high-caliber, market-driven team. Increased annual closing volume from $37.2M to $48.4M within 24 months. (CCC Software)
- Created, in one year, a proactive marketing program that increased positive media coverage 650%. (AAA Consulting)
- Boosted leads to 238 from less than 30 while cutting marketing costs 9%. (AAA Consulting)
- Led cross-functional team that cut costs 50% by implementing preconfigured hosting solutions. (BBB Software)
- Increased the identification-stage pipeline 239% and the qualified-stage pipeline 249% through Portfolio Management program. (SSS Consulting)
- Recruited 97 new accounts that delivered net revenue of $120K+ per month. (CCC Software)

CAREER TRACK

- Director, Sales Operations, AAA Consulting, Vancouver, BC	2006 – present
- Sales Manager, BBB Software, Toronto, ON	2005 – 2006
- Client Partner, SSS Consulting, Chicago, IL	2001 – 2005
- Business Development Manager, CCC Software, Montréal, QC	1999 – 2001

EDUCATION

- MBA, Purdue University – Krannert School of Management, West Lafayette, IN
- BS, University of Colorado, Boulder, CO – Computer Engineering

CRITICAL LEADERSHIP INITIATIVES

REIGNITING THE SALES OPERATIONS FUNCTION—AAA CONSULTING

Challenge #1   To turn around an underperforming operation; increase client-facing time for
                 salespeople; optimize lead generation; and field a more cost-effective sales group.

Actions   • Developed an overall operations framework.
                 • Created financial reporting and marketing metrics dashboard.
                 • Solidified negotiation and management vendor contracts, and built relation-
                   ships with unmatched loyalty.

Impact   Boosted leads from <30 to 238 while cutting costs 9%. Provided comprehen-
                 sive and rigorous reporting to drive maximum financial and marketing impact.
                 Achieved President's Club status.

Challenge #2   To transform sales efforts that were reactive rather than proactive and misaligned
                 with corporate objectives; to ensure intended audiences received consistent mes-
                 saging; and to reduce wasted man-hours and budget dollars resulting from weak
                 sales planning.

Actions   • Structured and implemented a strategy to increase market leadership.
                 • Developed and implemented objectives, operating procedures, sales training,
                   and budget.
                 • Leveraged social media, blogging, white papers, and response-based PR.

Impact   Increased positive media coverage 650% and reduced sales expenses 22%.

PROPELLING MARKETING SUCCESS—BBB SOFTWARE

Challenge #1   To facilitate the growth of the start-up North American Applications Management
                 System and Hosting practices. As Sales Manager, also accountable for sales
                 operations, training, and marketing.

Actions   • Wrote a comprehensive marketing/business-development plan.
                 • Launched an integrated high-touch lead generation campaign.
                 • Developed competitive analysis, collateral materials, and sales tools.

Impact   Successfully established the marketing and business development strategy plan,
                 resulting in a 100% increase in lead production. Collaborative efforts cut hosting
                 costs 50%.

You can take the targeted résumé a step further if you already have a "warm contact" inside the organization. This person might be a decision maker you know through your network or someone you've spoken to about the job. A warm contact is always a person whose priorities you understand. If you can, go around the normal application channels and send a highly targeted résumé to your contact.

A highly targeted résumé contains:

- A summary statement of the organization's problem.

- A proposed Contribution Statement.

- Background and experiences that show you can solve the organization's problem.

Here are two examples of a highly targeted résumé. The first comes from a very experienced, well-educated applicant, and the second from a recent college graduate looking for her first job. Both résumés are targeted at one prospect who has already explained the issues of concern to the applicant.

Highly Targeted Résumé 1

Marc Zeeman
marcz@helvmail.ch

15 Grunewaldstr CH4004
Basel, Switzerland

Telephone/Messages:
+41 61 425 70 0

At CodoPharm, it takes as long as two years for a new product application to be approved by the various medicine-control agencies such as the United States FDA. Every day out of the market costs about $2 million. With my background in improving regulatory processes, I would like to help CodoPharm reduce time to market by as much as 10 percent within three years.

How I have helped others:
Reduced average approval time at Milanoz from 20 months to 17 months. As director of regulatory documentation for three years, I instituted a "smart" Global Approval Process that met FDA requirements more precisely and cut review time by an average of 12 weeks. This translated into 60 days of market revenue, or roughly $24 million.

Gained $10 million in revenue for Grussli Pharmaceuticals through simultaneous submissions. Grussli was submitting drugs for approval in three different markets, one after the other. In my two years as regulatory officer, I created a process for simultaneous submissions, thus cutting about six months off approval times.

My educational background in this field:
Earned LL.M. in World Commerce Law, University of Bern. My thesis research was a comparison of legal requirements for drug approvals in Europe, the United States, and Japan. I developed a strong understanding of the nuances that can hinder approval across these different agencies.

Highly Targeted Résumé 2

Lia Mendoza
lialmend@opensource.com

46601 Boulder
Whittier, California 90602

Telephone/Messages:
(619) 555-7864

Dental Hygienist
Whittier Children's Dental Clinic is starting a new program to educate children and parents in preventive care. As a hygienist who is also a certified instructor in the Shining Smiles oral health curriculum, I believe I have the unique capability to provide excellent care and education to Whittier patients.

My background and education in this field:
Taught Shining Smiles oral health to more than 100 patients at Children's Hospital Los Angeles as a resident hygienist.

Certified in Shining Smiles curriculum at Concord College, San Ramon, CA. I learned the highly effective "Song and Story" approach to teaching preschool children how to care for their teeth. I participated in 12 student clinics to receive certification.

Delivered children's dental health presentations at the San Bernardino County health fair. More than 1200 people attended.

Certified Dental Hygienist, Concord College, San Ramon. My coursework included:

- Preventive education for pediatric patients.
- Dental procedures for oral examination, preventive, and restorative techniques.
- Four-handed, chair-side dentistry procedures.
- Preparation of restorative materials and models.
- Dental surgery preparation, administration of anesthetic, and suture removal.
- Cleaning and polishing techniques.

Resident Hygienist, Children's Hospital Los Angeles. In addition to conducting seminars as noted, assisted dentists and surgeons in routine procedures over a period of six months.

Member, Student Research Subgroup, Dental Hygiene Education Association. Participated in research projects on interdental brushes and laser dental cleaning.

Q: What should I put in a cover letter?

A: In your cover letter, introduce yourself and your résumé, tell why you're applying for the job, and ask for an interview. Many employers are more interested in your cover letter than your résumé because it tells them why you're applying and gives insight into your personality. As we've said, the purpose of a résumé is to obtain an interview, to start a conversation with the employer. Your cover letter is your opportunity to get that conversation under way—so we can't overemphasize the importance of the cover letter.

The worst thing you can do is write an offhand or "one size fits all" cover letter. You must target your cover letter to the specific needs and values of the prospective employer.

Ideally, your cover letter is a one-page proposal to fill an important business need you've identified in your research. Here is a basic format to follow:

1. Start by summing up the problem or opportunity your prospect faces and describe how you plan to help solve it. Use numbers that are meaningful to the prospect.

2. Give evidence that you can solve the problem and, if applicable, that you have solved one like it in the past. Evidence includes work and educational accomplishments that would lead your prospect to conclude you're right for the challenge.

3. Provide contact information and request a meeting.

Here is a sample cover letter:

Sample Cover Letter

Feb. 12, 2XXX

Haytham Arsad
Vice President, Marketing
Kali Palace Restaurants
7501 Bernard Ave.
Boston, MA 02110

Proposal to improve revenues and franchisee relationships as marketing liaison officer

Dear Mr. Arsad,

You have an opening for a marketing liaison officer with your franchisees. I would like to meet with you and show how I can fulfill your requirements.

Kali Palace has always had an excellent reputation among restaurant franchisees. Overall sales are flat, however, and some franchisees have expressed a desire for more marketing support from headquarters. My experience in conducting successful promotions leads me to suggest a way to improve revenues by at least 10 percent in one year and improve franchisee relationships at the same time.

In my three years at Niko's Gyros, I led an event-based marketing strategy that was credited with an annual 15 percent increase in revenues. We held monthly chain-wide promotions based on seasonal themes. The most successful were Spring Greek Salad Days, Lamb for Easter, and the fall Greek Festival.

Before that, over a five-year period at American Land restaurants, I successfully marketed and nearly doubled franchisee opportunities. The chain grew from 25 stores in 5 states to 47 stores in 14 states. One key to this success was a new 24/7 Web-based franchisee communication channel so that we could meet customer needs on a dime. We also simplified both menu offerings and advertising.

My resume is attached. I appreciate your taking the time to review my proposal. I'd like to present it to you in further detail. Please let me know when we can talk.

Sincerely,

Nuri Patel
4145 Bazar St.
Suffolk, MA 02104
(617) 555-0372
Nuripatel@sluzen.net

Q: I know I'm just one of a hundred applicants. How can I bypass the old application runaround and get an interview with the right person?

A: You've put your finger on a key issue. Your résumé is like an advertisement for a product that the employer might or might not want to buy. How do you treat unsolicited advertisements? Usually, they go into the trash.

Here's how it usually works in a large company. Your application and résumé might fall into an Applicant Tracking System, a computer that tells if you're using the right buzzwords. If not, you're automatically rejected. If you're lucky and get through the filter, someone (not the decision maker) will interview you. Then you'll be told, "We'll get back to you." Of course, as you say, hundreds of other people are going through the same process.

> Don't regard yourself as a product that needs a marketing brochure.... Consider yourself a living, breathing, intelligent problem solver.

Ideally, you stay completely out of this depressing loop. You don't regard yourself as a product that needs a marketing brochure. You consider yourself a living, breathing, intelligent problem solver. When that amazing job opportunity opens up, start your research. Next, you must get to the person with the power to hire you, and that requires taking initiative.

Find out who the decision maker is. Through research, find out what keeps that person awake at night. What key challenges or problems does the organization face? What do customers, suppliers, and reviewers say about the organization? Learn as much as you can.

Write a proposal letter introducing yourself and your solution. Ask for a few minutes to give a Need-Opportunity presentation. If possible, find someone—anyone—who can introduce you to the decision maker: a customer, a supplier, an insider, a board member. If you pay the price to make a strong business case for yourself, you have an excellent chance of getting the interview.

Even if you can't get to the decision maker, find someone on the inside who will commit to handing the decision maker your proposal. A hand-delivered proposal is far more compelling than a résumé that comes through the standard application system, and it stands a much greater chance of getting you that initial interview.

Of course, smaller companies might not have these elaborate systems for winnowing applicants, and it's usually much easier to reach the decision maker. Still, make the best business case you can.

You can use this approach to create a job, even when they're not hiring. If you can provide a compelling solution to a problem that matters to them, they'll find the resources to bring you on board.

Q: What are some ideas for a successful job interview?

A: Remember, you are a problem solver, not just a job seeker. When you make your appointment, ask if you can present a few ideas. Then pay the price to create a brief, hard-hitting Need-Opportunity presentation in which you demonstrate your knowledge of their issues and how you would deal with them.

By the time you get into the interview, you've already done so much research on their needs and concerns that you impress them with your understanding right away.

You are not passive. You go right to work. You are the proactive consultant who can help them with crucial challenges.

> Interviewers no longer ask if you have the skills they want — they now ask you to tell them about specific instances when you used your skills.

You might not feel comfortable about making a Need-Opportunity presentation in your first interview. You might not know enough about the company and their situation. In that case, use the first interview to prepare for a second interview, in which you will make a presentation.

Remember, the initial interview is just the beginning of a conversation. Ask the interviewer questions about issues you identified in your research. If your homework has uncovered a problem with, say, competitive pressures on the company, ask the interviewer his or her feelings about what you've heard. Use that first interview as a key research opportunity; then ask if you can return and make a brief proposal based on what you learn.

Interviewers no longer ask if you have the skills they want — they now want you to tell them about specific instances when you used your skills. For example, if your résumé says you have excellent communication skills, the interviewer will probably ask you about a time when you used those skills successfully. You should be prepared to tell a quick story about that experience.

But don't just answer the question. Find out *why* the interviewer cares about the question. When interviewers ask these usual generic interview questions, bring them back to their own concerns. For example, if they say, "Tell me about a time when you did this or that," answer briefly and then say, "It sounds like this issue is important to you. Could you tell me more about that?" For you, it's one more piece of crucial information.

MIT's Career Development Center suggests the "STAR" approach to interview questions: Situation, Task, Action, Result.[54] Prepare concise STARs for the typical interview questions you're likely to get. For example, the interviewer might say, "Tell us about a time you experienced conflict at work and how you resolved it." To prepare, think of a conflict situation you've experienced, what your task was, the action you took, and the result—the moral of the story.

When responding to the question, relate the situation—the first part of your STAR—and ask, "Is this the kind of thing you were looking for?"

Here's an example. The interviewer asks, "What is your key strength as a leader, and when did you capitalize on that strength?" A STAR response looks like this:

- (SITUATION) "My key strength is making informed decisions. I once led a sales group equally divided on whether we should have geographical sales territories or key accounts. It was a very political issue with people deeply invested on both sides."

- (TASK) "My task was to research the question and decide."

- (ACTION) "I found that key accounts would be much more productive, allowing a sales team to focus on one client regardless of geography, and I was able to sell that solution on the basis of my research."

- (RESULT) "We increased sales by a third the first year."

Then relate your STAR response to the challenges facing the interviewer's organization. And no matter what, don't ramble on, making the interviewer pick through everything you say for needed information. Practice answering questions concisely.

During the interview, periodically stop and ask, "Is this information helpful? Am I providing you with what you're looking for?" You'll show the interviewer that you care about others' point of view rather than fixating on your own agenda. Also, if you're going down the wrong path, you need this opportunity to course-correct.

Q: What does a Need-Opportunity presentation look like?

A: Start with the bottom line. What's the problem, and what benefit or solution can you bring to the problem? Make your solution as quantifiable as possible using charts with real numbers. Then go into the appropriate level of detail about each point of your solution.

Here's a sample outline of a Need-Opportunity presentation made by a person applying to be Site Safety Coordinator for a major commercial construction company.

Site incident rate high and costly...

- Your monthly incident rate: 131 reportable accidents.

- Insurance premiums will increase 20% this year if nothing is done.
- Productivity loss: running at 6% per project, high by industry standard (lost time, fines for safety violations, lawsuits).
- You must generate $74,000 per project just to cover these costs.

Where I've created a culture of safety...

- MacKay Homes, cut incident rate by 58% in one year.
- DJ Commercial Contractors, cut incident rate by 82% in three years.

How I create a culture of safety...

- Evaluate safety record of contractors, make it part of negotiation.
- Institute modular, frequent safety training instead of one class on entry.

Require supervisor accountability...

- Daily briefing on hazards.
- Mandatory compliance to safety-equipment checklist.

Next steps...

This simple outline, accompanied by charts showing the size of the problem and the benefit of the solution, demonstrates the real value this applicant brings. You can create something like this if you do your homework.

Occasionally, pause to ask your interviewer if your presentation is accurate and helpful. This will give him or her the chance to teach you more about the issue. If the interviewer feels your presentation is off track, stop and ask questions. Then offer to come back another time with a better presentation. Keep the conversation going.

Q: I've done what you suggest and I'm still out of a job. What now?

A: Then it's time to create your own job. Begin a blog. Make a podcast. Publish your own newsletter. With the experience and information you've gathered in researching and presenting yourself, you've become something of an expert in your field. So make a name for yourself. As people come to know about you, you will become a resource to them—a resource that ultimately someone will pay for.

This is also the time to fill your skills gap, which can in turn jump-start your job search. For example, communications specialist Laura Perry was out of work nearly a year. She realized that more and more openings in her field required exper-

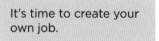
It's time to create your own job.

tise in social media that she didn't have. So she got busy learning about social media. She created a Facebook page for a friend's business, then volunteered to build Facebook and LinkedIn pages for a women's golf association. Soon she could talk knowledgeably about social media in job interviews and show samples of her work. A new job wasn't long in coming.[55]

Q: I already have a job, and I need to hold on to it. But I'm not very happy with it. Every day seems

about the same. I don't feel like I'm going anywhere careerwise.

A: Regardless of the job you have, you can grow to love your work and make a great career right where you are. It's a matter of your mindset.

That doesn't mean you should just "think positive." Instead, you should "think meaningful." How could you create out of your current job a new job that is far more significant to you and to your organization? A few suggestions:

- Write a Contribution Statement as described in this book. Share it with your manager and ask for input. Work it over together until you are both satisfied.

- Make a Win-Win Performance Agreement with your manager. Together, describe what would be a win for the organization and a win for you personally. Define the guidelines you need to follow, resources you'll need, and how you will account to each other for progress.

- Set clear goals with your manager. Use this formula to state the goal: "From X to Y by When." Here's a charge nurse's example: "I will improve patient satisfaction in my unit from 80 percent to 95 percent by the end of the fiscal year." By achieving clear goals, you demonstrate your value and you find out what it feels like to win.

- If your employer does quarterly or yearly performance reviews, ask if you can have mini-reviews at least monthly. A few minutes with your manager once or twice a month can be far more useful in improving your performance than an hour once a year.

Q: I keep hearing you say, "Create your own job." But what if the job description is very clear and you don't really need to go beyond it?

A: There are two mindsets about work. The Industrial Age mind says, "I'm a machine with a specific function." The other is the Knowledge Age mind, which says, "I'm a creative, living, thinking human being with unique gifts. No one else can do what I do." The Industrial Age worker, like a machine, wears out and is easily replaced, just as you would replace a car, a computer, or a toaster that doesn't fit your needs anymore. The knowledge worker is by definition irreplaceable. No matter what job you're in, you must constantly be re-creating it, or you become irrelevant pretty fast.

> Some people have to climb the mountain from the bottom up, while others get helicoptered to the top.

Of course, you must fulfill the requirements of your job description. But the real question is, "How is this job different because you are the one doing it?"

Q: It's easy to get a job if you're rich and well connected. But what if I'm just starting out, I have nothing, and nobody knows me?

A: It's true that some people have to climb the mountain from the bottom up, while others get helicoptered to the top. And the mountain can look steep and impassable to you. But remember who you are. You're not nobody. You're a unique package of talents, passion, and conscience that exists nowhere else. You can cut your own path up the mountain, and even though you might get stuck for a while or even slip backwards, the strength you gain by making your own way will more than offset the weakness of the "easy rider" who gets a free pass to the summit.

There are natural principles at work here. An easy ride produces little strength of character or capability. If you're the one who takes the tough climb, you will naturally outperform the privileged ones — or if not, you will still have a far more meaningful career than they can ever have. How many successful people have come from difficult beginnings — from Oprah Winfrey to numerous well-known CEOs to your neighbor who is the first in her family to own a home?

Take the initiative. If you can't get an interview, you just haven't made the right case to the right people yet. Keep working at it. If your boss doesn't notice you, start working in your Circle of Influence and watch it expand. It might be slowgoing, but if you persist, you'll become more influential, gain more resources and respect, and create the great career you want.

Closing Thoughts

As you look around at your career prospects, you might see nothing encouraging, like the visitors to Yellowstone after the 1988 fires. But recall that those who saw only disaster didn't see things as they really were. That barren landscape was filled with hidden potential for growth. The same is true for your career, even in challenging times. Possibilities abound on all sides. The only shortage of opportunity is in your mind.

In fact, the opportunities could not be greater for those who adopt the right paradigm.

The old Industrial Age paradigm tells you that you're at the mercy of the economy, the industry, the boss, the job description, the standard operating procedure, and everything else that makes you a victim. If you continue to suffer under that paradigm, your relevance, your job security, and even your personal fulfillment and health are at stake.

On the other hand, if you adopt the Knowledge Age paradigm, you free yourself. You don't look for a job;

you look for a significant problem to solve or an exciting opportunity to leverage. You look for a profession you love and that people will pay you to do. You are not a "job description with legs," but a thinking, creative human being with unique and irreplaceable talents. You can make a contribution no one else can make.

The prominent business thinker Jim Collins observes, "It is impossible to have a great life unless it is a meaningful life. And it is very difficult to have a meaningful life without meaningful work."[56] It doesn't matter if you're the CEO or the office cleaner or a police officer or a teacher or a lawyer or a waiter or a homemaker or a movie star. It doesn't matter what you do. Your career will be great if you make it great.

Notes

1. You can watch a video about Fiona Wood at www.franklincovey.com/greatcareer.

2. "Dr. Fiona Wood Is the Most Trusted Australian," Australian of the Year Awards, Jun. 30, 2008. http://www.australianoftheyear.org.au/media/?view=news&id=579. Accessed Oct. 2, 2009.

3. "Dr. Fiona Wood: Australian of the Year," *Platypus Magazine*, Oct. 2005, 3–4.

4. "Microsoft Australia Congratulates Australian of the Year," Jan. 25, 2005. http://www.microsoft.com/australia/presspass/news/pressreleases/Ausofyear.mspx. Accessed Aug. 20, 2009.

5. A. Roger and Rebecca Merrill, *Life Matters*, McGraw-Hill, 2004, 62.

6. Sandra Block, "Traditional Company Pensions Are Going Away Fast," *USA Today*, May 21, 2009.

7. Thomas Davenport, *Thinking for a Living*, Harvard Business School Press, 2005, 62.

8. Edgar Johnson, "*A Christmas Carol* Criticizes England's Economic System," *Readings on Charles Dickens*, ed. Clarice Swisher, Greenhaven Press, 1997, 86–93.

9. Kate Flint, *The Victorian Novelist: Social Problems and Social Change*, Routledge, 1987, 234.

10. Peter Hawkins and Nick Smith, *Coaching, Mentoring, and Organizational Consultancy*, Open University Press, 2007, 45.

11. "Katherine Bicer," *Engineer Your Life*, http://www.engineeryourlife.org/cms/6198.aspx. Accessed Sep. 2, 2009.

12. Natasha Chilingerian, "The Winning Doc: Beauty queen-turned-physician," *American Press*, Jun. 20, 2007.

13. Brian Ness, http://mehs.d.umn.edu/. Accessed Sep. 2, 2009.

14. Dylan Klempner, *American Chestnuts* DVD, Massachusetts Association of the American Chestnut Foundation.

15. Julia Tang Peters, "Leadership Effectiveness Quotient," http://www.lequotient.com. Accessed Sep. 1, 2009.

16. Taylor Mali, "What Teachers Make," cited by Thomas Friedman, "Listen to Your Heart," Commencement Address, Williams College, Williamstown, MA, Jun. 5, 2005 . http://www.humanity.org/voices/commencements/speeches/index.php?page=friedman_at_williams. Accessed Sep. 1, 2009.

17. Cited in Stephen R. Covey, *The 8th Habit: From Effectiveness to Greatness*, Free Press, 2004, 70.

18. Steven Falkenberg, "Factors in Employee Motivation/Satisfaction," Eastern Kentucky University, 1997. http://people.eku.edu/falkenbergs/motive.htm. Accessed Sep. 2, 2009.

19. Charles Handy, *The Age of Paradox*, Harvard Business Press, 1995, 6.

20. Charles Handy, *The Elephant and the Flea*, Harvard Business Press, 2003, 3.

21. Richard Florida, "How the Crash Will Reshape America," *The Atlantic*, Mar 2009, 51.

22. *Daily Wisdom: 365 Buddhist Inspirations*, ed. Josh Bartok, Wisdom Publications, 2001.

23. Roger Boyes, "Forget Burnout, Boreout Is the New Office Disease," *Times Online*, Sep. 15, 2007.

24. Cited in Handy, *Paradox*, 17–18.

25. Handy, *Paradox*, 20.

26. Richard Koch, *The 80/20 Principle*, Doubleday, 1999, 174.

27. Julia Child, *My Life in France*, Anchor Books, 2007, 19, 59, 146.

28. Jim Collins, *How the Mighty Fall*, Harper-Collins, 2009, 57.

29. Liane Hansen and Laura Krantz, "Remembering the 1988 Yellowstone Fires," *Yellowstone: Evolution of a National Treasure*, National Public Radio, 31 Aug. 2008, http://www.npr.org/templates/story/story.php?storyId=94126845.

30. Brian X. Chen, "iPhone Developers Go From Rags to Riches," *Wired*, Sep. 19, 2008.

31. Linda Franklin, "iPhone Millionaires—The Making of an App," Examiner.com, Apr. 8, 2009.

32. Cathy Free, "A Mother Finds Calling Beyond Her Own Border," *Deseret News*, Mar. 11, 2004.

33. James J. Asher, *Learning Another Language Through Actions*, Sky Oaks Productions, 1982; "Language by Command," *The Way of Learning*, Summer 1984, 35. http://www.context.org/ICLIB/IC06/Asher.htm.

34. Sarah E. Needleman, "Giving a Stalled Job Search a Jump-Start," *The Wall Street Journal*, Oct. 20, 2009, D8.

35. David Meerman Scott, *World Wide Rave: Creating Triggers That Get Millions of People to Spread Your Ideas and Share Your Stories*, Wiley, 2009, 40.

36. Steve Rubel, "The Most Essential Career Skill You Need to Succeed," http://www.micropersuasion.com/2007/05/the_most_essent.html. Accessed Oct. 20, 2009.

37. Carol Eikleberry, *The Career Guide for Creative and Unconventional People*, Ten Speed Press, 2004, 35.

38. Eikleberry, *Career Guide*, ix.

39. Sylvia Nasar, "The Top Draft Pick in Economics: A Professor to Be Coveted by Two Dozen Universities," *The New York Times*, Apr. 21, 1995. Italics ours.

40. Richard Louv, "Hope in Hell's Classroom," *The New York Times Magazine*, Nov. 25, 1990, 30.

41. Barbara K. Schell and Molly C. Curren, "A Human in Action," 4. humanityinaction.org. Accessed Sep. 2, 2009.

42. "Aurora Ill. Police Officer Named Police Officer of the Year 2008," *International Assn. of Chiefs of Police*, Nov. 6, 2008. www.theiacp.org/About/Awards. Accessed Sep. 2, 2009.

43. Peter Drucker, *Management Challenges for the 21st Century*, Harper-Collins, 2002, 187.

44. From *The Gift: Poems by Hafiz*, trans. Daniel Ladinsky, Penguin Compass, 1999, 117.

45. Joseph McBride, *Steven Spielberg*, Simon & Schuster, 2008, 111.

46. Tom Powers, *Steven Spielberg*, Lerner Publications, 2007, 7.

47. Marcus Buckingham and Curt Coffman, *First, Break All the Rules*, Simon & Schuster, 1999, 37.

48. Sarah Childress, "A Young Tinkerer Builds a Windmill, Electrifying a Nation," *The Wall Street Journal*, Dec. 12, 2007. See also William's blog at http://williamkamkwamba.type-pad.com. Accessed Oct. 8, 2009.

49. Cited in Stanley Fish, *Doing What Comes Naturally*, Duke University Press, 1990, 201.

50. Lance Haun, "How Having a Blog Landed Me a New Job," Aug. 3, 2009. http://rehaul.com/blogging-leads-to-job-opportunities. Accessed Oct. 8, 2009.

51. Cited in Scott, *World Wide Rave*, 42.

52. See Damian Counsell's blog at http://weddingphotography-blog.com. Accessed Oct. 5, 2009.

53. Katie Hafner and Matthew Lyon, *Where Wizards Stay Up Late: The Origins of the Internet*, Simon & Schuster, 1998, 79.

54. "STAR Method," MIT Career Development Center, http://web.mit.edu/career/www/guide/star.html. Accessed Oct. 9, 2009.

55. Needleman, "Stalled Job Search," D8.

56. Jim Collins, *Good to Great: Why Some Companies Make the Leap... and Others Don't*, Harper Business, 2001, 210.

Index

80/20 Principle– 40

A

Abundance vs. scarcity paradigm– 51, 52, 54, 57
A Christmas Carol– 15, 152
Anthony, Susan B.– 23
Apple– 121
Asher, James– 55, 56
Athey, Susan– 61, 62, 63

B

Babber, Vidushi– 17
Baran, Paul– 124
Bicer, Katherine– 16, 153

C

Cartwright, Madeline– 75, 77, 78
Chazin, Steve– 121
Child, Julia– 41, 42, 43, 154
Clark Medal– 62
Collins, Jim– 44, 48, 151, 154, 156
Contribution Statement, how to write– 78–87
Cordon Bleu school– 42

K

M

N

O

P

R

Acknowledgments

This book would not have been possible without the contributions of many of our friends and FranklinCovey family members. We thank Sean Covey, Adam Merrill, Annie Oswald, Stephan Mardyks, Sam Bracken, Todd Davis, Janita Anderson, Will Colosimo, Tamara Davies, Gil Wilburn, and Boyd Craig for their helpful reviews of the manuscript.

We were fortunate to have the input of the highly professional employment coaches at the Utah Department of Workforce Services—Steve Leyba, Karla Aguirre, and particularly Cathy Carey—who have helped thousands of people succeed in building the career they want.

Thanks goes to the FranklinCovey production staff: Jody Karr, Andrea McCloy, RJ Venkatapathy, James Boley, and particularly Jenny Lloyd, who coordinated the book project. Editing help came from Reid Later and marketing and publication-relations assistance from Debra Lund. Finally, we are grateful to Breck England for his help in writing the manuscript.

About the Authors

Dr. Stephen R. Covey is an internationally respected leadership authority, teacher, author, organizational consultant, and co-founder and vice chairman of FranklinCovey Co. He is author of *The 7 Habits of Highly Effective People*, which *Chief Executive* magazine has called the most influential business book of the last 100 years. The book has sold nearly 20 million copies, and after 20 years, still holds a place on most best-seller lists.

Dr. Covey earned an MBA from Harvard and a doctorate from BYU, where he was a professor of organizational behavior. For more than 40 years, he has taught millions of people—including leaders of nations and corporations—the transforming power of the principles that govern individual and organizational effectiveness. He and his wife live in the Rocky Mountains of Utah.

Jennifer Colosimo is the Chief Learning Officer at Franklin-Covey Co. Jennifer has influenced more than 30,000 clients globally through her facilitation and keynotes. She is an executive coach and a catalyst for high performance at all organizational levels, from frontline to CEO.

Before joining FranklinCovey in 1996, Jennifer earned an MA in organizational communication from Purdue University and served as a change management consultant with Accenture. For FranklinCovey, she has facilitated many audio and Web-based programs, including the iTunes series "Greatness on the Go" and the webinar series "The Speed of Trust," and has co-hosted leadership events with such luminaries as Jack Welch and her coauthor, Stephen R. Covey. Jennifer lives in sunny Colorado with her husband and daughters.

About FranklinCovey

FranklinCovey (NYSE: FC) is the global consulting and training leader in the areas of strategy execution, customer loyalty, leadership, and individual effectiveness. Clients include 90 percent of the Fortune 100, more than 75 percent of the Fortune 500, thousands of small- and mid-sized businesses, as well as numerous government entities and educational institutions. FranklinCovey has 46 direct and licensee offices providing professional services in 147 countries.

FranklinCovey offers training in the following areas:

- Leadership Development
- The 7 Habits
- Time Management
- Customer Loyalty
- Strategy Consulting
- Communication
- Project Management
- Diversity
- Sales Performance

For more information, go to www.franklincovey.com/tc.

About FranklinCovey Services

On-Site Consulting, Training, and Keynotes

Based all over the world, our consultants represent diverse, global industry experience and tailor their delivery to your precise needs—whether consulting, training, or customized keynotes. Our consultants deliver results at any level, from the C-suite to a team or department.

Client-Facilitator Certification

For organizations seeking cost-effective ways to implement solutions involving large populations of managers and frontline workers, FranklinCovey certifies on-site client facilitators to teach our material and adapt it to your organization's needs. We have certified more than 25,000 client facilitators worldwide.

Open-Enrollment Public Programs

For organizations needing professional development for a dispersed workforce or education for individuals, FranklinCovey offers nearly 1,200 open-enrollment programs to the public in 120 metropolitan areas throughout the United States. Similar programs are offered throughout the world by our regional and local offices.

Custom Solutions

When clients have a unique learning or delivery need, FranklinCovey can customize its solutions. We can provide:

- Tailored FranklinCovey training programs.
- Customized planners and binders.
- Specific tools, guides, and other implementation aids.
- Simulations, games, case studies, and other unique learning approaches.

Content Licensing

For organizations that desire to implement solutions, by division or companywide, in a cost-effective way, FranklinCovey will license your organization to use our content or intellectual property in whatever way you see fit. This provides you with ultimate flexibility and scalability.

FranklinCovey Online Learning

FranklinCovey Online Learning products and solutions give you the benefits of our world-class training and the convenience of online delivery—along with compelling content, award-winning videos, and live engagement.

LiveClicks webinar workshops put the high-quality instruction of FranklinCovey in-person training into convenient online workshops. LiveClicks webinar workshops are led by our certified instructors, or yours, and are presented live online in two-hour modules. Engaging and interactive, LiveClicks webinar workshops offer compelling content and award-winning videos. Learn more at: **www.franklincovey.com/liveclicks.**

Help teams take action for increased performance with FranklinCovey InSights. InSights are short, Web-based, video-rich learning modules based on core competencies, delivered in the course of regularly held meetings by your own managers or leaders. Each InSights module starts with an engaging video, followed by powerful discussion questions. Our online forum and goal-tracking tool further help teams learn and develop. Learn more at: **www.franklincovey.com/insights.**

Develop effective employees and build cohesive teams, no matter what the person's role, with *The 7 Habits of Highly Effective People—Interactive Edition*. Based on the best-selling business book and our world-class effectiveness workshops, *The 7 Habits Interactive Edition* is a three-hour, self-paced online experience, with an optional one-day live session available for a blended learning experience.

Learn more at: **www.franklincovey.com/the7habitsinteractive.**

For more information contact a FranklinCovey Online Learning Specialist at: 1-888-576-1776.

Books and Audio

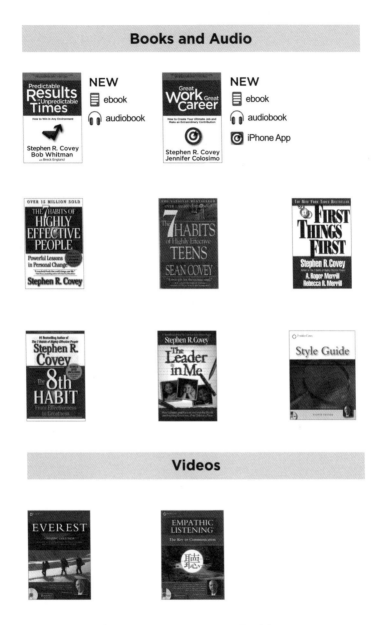

NEW
- ebook
- audiobook

NEW
- ebook
- audiobook
- iPhone App

Videos

For more information, go to www.franklincovey.com/tc.